# Baking with Einkorn
# Modern Recipes for an Ancient Grain
*Featuring "Better-for-You" Ingredients*

## Diana Konkle

Food Styling & Photography
by Annette Riese

Graphic Design & Layout
by Debra Riedel

## American Printing Company
Madison, Wisconsin

© 2016 by Diana Konkle

Food Styling & Photography © 2016 by Annette Riese

All rights reserved

Printed in the United States by
American Printing Company
Madison, Wisconsin

Reproduction in whole or in part of any portion, in any form, without permission is prohibited.

Outcomes may vary due to oven temperature accuracy and the proprietary milling process of the Einkorn flour resource used. The author is not responsible for any adverse effects arising directly or indirectly as a result of the information provided in this book. You are advised to consult with your family physician regarding your family's nutrition, health and wellness.

First Edition

9 8 7 6 5 4 3 2 1
Digit on the right indicates the number of this printing.

ISBN-13: 978-0-692-78340-5

ISBN-10: 0-692-78340-7

To order additional copies of this book email us at:
bakingwitheinkorn@gmail.com

*Also ask at your local bookstore!*

# Dedication

To Mom, my first teacher - you nurtured my love of the kitchen!

# Contents

Welcome .................................................................. I
My Story ................................................................ III

## Part I: Better-for-You Baking

Baking with Einkorn ............................................. V
Baking with Less Sugar ...................................... VIII
Baking with Essential Oils ..................................... X
Adding Color to Baked Goods ............................ XI

## Part II: Pantry Makeover

Pantry Organization ........................................... XII
Pantry Ingredients ............................................ XIII
Tools & Equipment ........................................... XVI

## Part III: Recipes

Cookies ................................................................ 1
Breads & Pastries ............................................... 19
Pies & Tarts ........................................................ 41
Cakes & Cupcakes ............................................. 55
Healthy Snacks & Bars ...................................... 73
Miscellaneous Fun ............................................. 87

Acknowledgements ......................................... 102
Index ................................................................ 106

# Welcome to my kitchen!

In this cookbook, I have converted over 50 of my family-favorite bakery recipes into better-for-you versions. Over the last few years, I have realized the effect that processed sugar and flour have had on my health. This started me on a mission to change not only my diet, but to help raise awareness in others of what is in many of the bakery and snack items they eat today.

Baking from scratch is a lost art. Many people have never been taught how to bake; therefore, they purchase and consume unhealthy commercialized snacks and baked goods. For those who do bake, the difficultly is knowing which ingredients are best to use. Many of the ingredients on the market today are not the same as those that were used when I was growing up; they are highly processed, chemically enhanced, and contain an abundance of sugar.

My goal is to guide you on which ingredients to use and to provide you with delicious foolproof recipes. I will introduce you to Einkorn flour, an ancient grain that is a key ingredient in my recipes. In comparison to modern hybridized wheat, Einkorn has a simple gluten structure, making it easier to digest and often tolerated by gluten-sensitive individuals. I also focus on reducing the amount of refined sugar in my baked goods. I will share with you tips and guidelines I use to reduce sugar in my recipes without compromising taste.

I hope the success you meet with each recipe will give you confidence in your baking skills and inspire you to spend more time baking in your kitchen!

*Diana Konkle*

# My Story

## Childhood Memories

My passion for baking began as a child in my mother's and grandmothers' kitchens. I have fond memories of watching their skilled hands, learning their techniques, and acquiring confidence in my baking skills. Pies and cinnamon rolls were both of my grandmothers' specialties, and my mother was a master at the art of baking bread. For my family, the kitchen was the heart of our home; where we ate wonderful food, conversed and learned many life lessons.

## Teaching Career

Teaching Home Economics was a natural career choice for me. I earned a BA in Foods and Nutrition from the University of Northern Iowa and taught at the high school level four years. I enjoyed inspiring my students and helping them meet success in the kitchen. Throughout the years, many of them have reconnected with me to share heart-warming memories about their time in my classroom and to share their personal cooking and baking experiences. When my first child was born, I put my teaching career on hold.

## Specialty Shop Venture

When my children entered grade school, I launched *The Confection Connection*, a specialty candy-making supply shop that evolved into a bakery, deli, catering, and tearoom business. For 24 years, I sweetened Sun Prairie's citizens with my handmade confections, scratch bakery, deli lunches, and catered entrees. To this day, customers reminisce about their favorite items and recreate them, using my first cookbook, *Favorite Recipes from Diana's Confection Connection*, as their guide.

## Wake-Up Call

Two months after I sold my business, my husband became very ill. During this dark time, I came to the realization that *if you do not have your health, nothing else matters*. I began to analyze my own health. I had gained 75 pounds, had trouble sleeping, and had minor digestive issues. Many of my friends were being diagnosed with serious medical conditions and I was concerned health issues would happen to me next.

I made the decision to be proactive about my own health. I began to examine my diet and enrolled in a nutrition and wellness program. I became aware that sugar and flour, the two most prominent ingredients in my bakery, were the probable cause of my health issues. When I eliminated them from my diet, my health issues began to disappear and weight loss was my only side effect! This is when I became determined to live a healthier, cleaner life.

## Lessons Learned

- The body is a magnificent machine. Respect your body. Appreciate all of the functions performed daily to keep you alive.

- Every day there are opportunities to learn something new and sharing this knowledge can be very powerful.

- The power of nature is magnificent. When given proper nourishment, the body often has the ability to heal itself.

- Health is the real wealth of life! Without your health, you have nothing.

- Initiate lifestyle changes to improve your health. Inspire others to do the same. One of the greatest joys is to watch others thrive.

That is my story and that is why I now devote my energy and time to learning and teaching wellness. I hope you are inspired to get in your kitchen, to use healthy ingredients, and to bake! Let this cookbook be your guide and discover that the kitchen is the place where true health begins.

# Baking with Einkorn Flour

On my quest to create healthy bakery, I experimented with numerous flour alternatives. I discovered that with many of these ingredients, it was necessary to use fillers such as cornstarch, potato starch, tapioca starch, and xanthan gum in order to simulate the baking properties of modern wheat. Many of these filler ingredients are high in carbohydrates and calories and the finished products containing these ingredients have an unsatisfactory taste, texture, and/or appearance. However, when I began to test Einkorn flour in my recipes, I was encouraged by the results and intrigued by the nutritional benefits. Through experimentation, I learned to work with Einkorn's unique characteristics and I was able to successfully reformulate my favorite recipes.

## What is Einkorn Wheat?

Einkorn wheat was one of the first plants to be cultivated over 10,000 years ago, and grew long before that. All varieties of modern wheat are hybridized descendants of wild Einkorn wheat. Einkorn wheat has one grain attached to its stem, while other forms of wheat have four grains attached to their stems. The term "einkorn" is derived from the German language and interpreted to mean "single grain." Einkorn wheat grows slowly, has small yields, and is difficult to harvest; therefore, was abandoned until recent health-seeking individual started to take interest in Einkorn's nutritional profile.

## How Does Einkorn Differ from Modern Wheat?

Throughout history, wheat has been cultivated and hybridized to increase yield, to increase disease resistance, and to develop desirable baking characteristics. As a result, modern wheat is very different than ancient Einkorn. The genetic makeup of modern wheat is more complex than that of Einkorn; Einkorn contains 14 chromosomes and modern varieties contain 42 chromosomes. Einkorn is not gluten-free, but has a simple gluten structure that is often tolerated by gluten-sensitive individuals. I have noticed with my gluten sensitivity, I am able to eat Einkorn without any digestive issues. Additionally, I think Einkorn is much tastier than modern wheat and I feel more satisfied after eating a bakery item made with Einkorn flour.

The nutritional profile of Einkorn is compelling. Einkorn is about 50% higher in protein than modern wheat and has 3 to 4 times more riboflavin, beat-carotene, and lutein.  Einkorn is also a great source of minerals including zinc, manganese, potassium, phosphorus, and iron. (Einkorn.com. Accessed May 15, 2016. http://www.einkorn.com/wp-content/upload/2009/12/Grain-Nutrition-Comparison-Matrix.pdf)

Having grown up on an Iowa farm, I have observed firsthand how farming techniques have changed over the last 50 years. More fertilizers, pesticides, and other chemicals are used in the production of today's wheat; and synthetic nutrients are added to enrich the flour to compensate for nutrition that has been lost through genetic modification and through modern harvesting and milling techniques.  The flour my grandmas and mom had in their pantries was not the same as the flour that is available today!

## Where Can You Purchase Einkorn Flour?

Einkorn is slowly becoming available at specialty grocery stores and independent supplement and wellness providers.  You can also buy Einkorn flour online.

There are three kinds of Einkorn flour on the market today: whole grain Einkorn flour, bolted Einkorn flour, and all-purpose Einkorn flour.  All of these flours are milled from the same Einkorn berries.  Whole grain Einkorn flour contains all of the grain's bran and germ and has a hearty dense texture and a slightly nutty flavor.  In bolted Einkorn flour, a portion of the bran has been sifted out, making it ideal when you need a lighter flour, yet desire the nutritional benefits of the germ.  All-purpose Einkorn flour is milled to have the majority of bran and germ removed, perfect for applications that require a fine, delicate texture.  Each type of Einkorn flour has slightly different baking characteristics and results vary.  I like to use a combination of these flours in some of my recipes.  I suggest you experiment with the different types of Einkorn flour and decide what you like.  Since Einkorn is minimally processed, staling occurs quickly.  To extend shelf life, store in sealed containers and refrigerate or freeze.

Einkorn flour may seem expensive; the price reflects the fact that this ancient grain is more difficult for farmers to grow and harvest than modern wheat.  I was cost-conscious when I reformulated my recipes; I often blend Einkorn flour with some of my favorite less expensive ingredients that compliment Einkorn's unique taste, texture, and structure.  I have great appreciation for the farmers who are dedicated to the revival of Einkorn, enabling consumers like me to enjoy the distinctive nutrition and health benefits of this grain.

## Tips and Guidelines

Einkorn flour can be substituted for modern all-purpose flour in most recipes; however, adjustments to ingredient ratios and modifications to preparation techniques are required because of Einkorn's simple gluten structure. I have come to realize that the final results may not always be quite the same as when modern wheat is used, and I have adjusted my recipes and standards to reflect Einkorn's unique texture and characteristics.

1. Einkorn absorbs liquids and fats more slowly than traditional flour. I have found that allowing the dough or batter to "rest" 10-15 minutes before baking, gives the flour extra time to absorb these ingredients. In many recipes, I have also decreased the amount of liquids by 15-20%.

2. Batter containing Einkorn should be "worked" as little as possible. Be careful not to over-mix the ingredients. Over-mixing activates stickiness. Most of my recipes instruct you to "stir until just combined."

3. Yeast dough containing Einkorn flour requires less kneading than dough containing modern wheat. The dough is also less elastic and does not rise as much. Over-proofing can result in the dough collapsing in the oven.

4. Almond flour compliments Einkorn flour in cookie formulations. I use 1 part almond flour to 2 parts Einkorn in many of my recipes.

5. Oat flour provides a wholesome dimension of flavor to breakfast bakery. I use equal parts of oat flour and Einkorn flour in a variety of my recipes.

# Baking with less Sugar

There are many different types of sugar, and sugar is added to many processed foods. Even if you are a label-reader, it may be difficult to know if a product contains added sugar. As a consumer, you may feel like manufacturers are trying to cleverly disguise sugar in their products by using unfamiliar names in their ingredient statements.

Bakery, snack foods, and commercial beverages tend to contain high amounts of sugar. These are items that I used to consume frequently. When I learned that *1 gram of sugar is equivalent to 4 teaspoons of sugar*, I realized I was consuming nearly 1 cup of sugar a day! This was a life-changing moment for me. This is when I decided to reduce my intake of sugar, an ingredient to which I had become addicted.

When you make your own bakery and snacks, you know exactly what is in them. There are many ways to decrease the amount of sugar you add to a recipe. Your taste buds will adjust to lower levels of sweetness and you will begin to enjoy the flavor qualities of other ingredients. To prevent overindulgence, make recipes with smaller yields or portion your goodies into smaller servings.

## Tips and Guidelines

When creating recipes for this cookbook, my priority was to reformulate each recipe to contain less sugar than the original. I discovered for most recipes that I could reduce the amount of refined sugar by at least half. Here are techniques I used to accomplish this:

1. Honey, maple syrup, and coconut sugar tend to have a more intense sweetness compared to refined sugar; therefore, less is needed to achieve the same sweetness. I use a combination of honey and coconut sugar in many of my recipes.

2. Fruits and vegetables add a natural sweetness to recipes. Bananas, apples, blueberries, zucchini, carrots, and pumpkin puree are some that I like to use.

3. Dried fruits also provide sweetness. Be sure to read package labels and avoid brands with added sugar.

4. Chocolate contributes a fudgy, buttery flavor to recipes. Use chocolates that are high in cacao; they contain less sugar.

5. Butter, coconut oil, and olive oil add flavor to bakery and contribute to surface browning.

6. Flavorings and spices are a great way to add flavor to baked goods. Increase the amount of these ingredients to compensate for the reduction of sugar.

7. Frostings and many commercially-made decorations contain sugar. Cut back on the amount you use on cakes, cupcakes, and muffins.

# Baking with Essential Oils

Essential oils are pure and can add concentrated flavor to your baked goods. They are a great alternative to artificial extracts and a wonderful substitution when fresh herbs are not available.

## Tips and Guidelines

1. Use brands that are therapeutic, certified organic, or wild crafted for baking. Some of my favorites are: cinnamon bark, ginger, clove, nutmeg, lemon, lime, orange, peppermint, black pepper, rosemary, thyme, and basil.

2. Essential oils are extremely concentrated. In my recipes, I provide a suggested usage range; start with a drop or two and then adjust to taste. Use a toothpick to control the addition of smaller amounts; dip the toothpick into the oil and then stir into food.

3. Temperature affects the stability of essential oils. You may need to add a bit more to account for any oil that evaporates during baking.

4. Use only glass bowls when baking with essential oils. Oils tend to cling to metal and leach toxins from plastic.

5. Store essential oils away from heat and light to extend shelf life.

6. Make sure to recap your bottles to prevent evaporation and spilling.

7. Give baked goods a subtle hint of flavor by applying essential oils topically after baking. In a 4-ounce trigger bottle, add a few drops of essential oil to 2 tablespoons of olive oil, and fill to top with distilled water. Spray mixture onto crackers, breads, and chips.

# Adding Color to Baked Goods

We eat with our mouths, but our eyes tell us if something looks appealing. Color often makes baked goods look more appetizing. Do not be tempted to use artificial food dyes to color your treats. There are many natural ways to add a spark of color to your goodies. I think you will agree that the natural colors provided by fruits, vegetables, and spices are beautiful and more mouth-watering than artificial ones.

## Tips and Guidelines

1. Use Natural Rainbow Sprinkles to add a fun spark of color to cookies, cakes, and donuts. My recipe can be found on page 15. Visually comparable to store-bought sprinkles, my sprinkles are made from ground unsweetened flaked coconut that is naturally colored with vegetables and spices. Make several batches, which you can freeze so you always have some on hand.

2. Use dehydrated fruits to add color to frostings, glazes, and whipped toppings. I invite you to refer to my recipe for Strawberry Cream Cheese Frosting on page 68 and my recipe for Berry Whipped Coconut Cream on page 98.

# Pantry Makeover

Principles I learned in a kitchen management course over fifty years ago still apply today. Let me guide you on how to organize your pantry, educate you on the ingredients you should purchase to fill that pantry, and recommend basic kitchen tools and equipment. When your makeover is complete, you will have everything you need to make the recipes in this cookbook.

## Pantry Organization

1. **Clean out the old stuff.**
   Go through the items in your cupboards and get rid of the ingredients that have expired or that you don't use anymore.

2. **Find the right storage containers.**
   An organized pantry is easier to use than a cluttered one. Decide which storage options work best for you and your space. I use recycled bulk nut containers to store my flours and sugars. They are uniform is size, have airtight lids, and fit well in my storage area. I have found that baskets work well for storing bags of dried fruit, nuts, and spices.

3. **Label your ingredients.**
   Write ingredient names and best by dates on your storage containers. I can't tell you how many times I've put something in a container and forgotten what is in that container or when I bought it!

4. **Store similar items together.**
   Keep your canned goods together on a shelf; keep your spices together in a basket. When similar items are stored together, they are easier to find.

5. **Prioritize items by frequency of use.**
   Put ingredients that you use all of the time near the front of your cupboards where they can be quickly grabbed. Try to store these ingredients near your preparation space.

## Pantry Ingredients

**All Purpose-Einkorn Flour** is milled to remove the majority of the bran and germ. All-purpose Einkorn flour has a very smooth and fine texture, yielding a sweet, delicate crumb when used in cookies, muffins, cakes, and quick breads. To maintain freshness, store in an airtight container in the refrigerator or freezer.

**Whole Grain Einkorn Flour** retains all the bran and germ in the milling process. Whole grain Einkorn flour is hearty and has a slightly nutty flavor and delivers a tender, wholesome, and satisfying texture. To maintain freshness, store in an airtight container in the refrigerator or freezer.

**Bolted Einkorn Flour** is a whole grain flour with a portion of the bran sifted out, making this flour a nice compromise between the hearty whole grain Einkorn flour and the all-purpose Einkorn flour. Bolted Einkorn flour is ideal when you want a lighter flour, yet wish to maintain the nutrition found in the germ. To maintain freshness, store in an airtight container in the refrigerator or freezer.

**Almond Flour** is made from skinless, blanched almonds that have been finely ground. Almond flour is gluten-free, makes baked goods moist, contributes a rich buttery flavor, and blends well with Einkorn flour in cookie recipes.

**Old-Fashioned Oats/Oat Flour** is a high-fiber, gluten-free grain that adds great texture and nutrition to a recipe. You can make oat flour by blending old-fashioned oats in a food processor until finely ground. Organic oatmeal provides assurance that no chemicals or pesticides have been used during production.

. . . . . . . . . . . . . . . . . . . . . . . . . . . . . . . . . . . . . . . . . . . . . . . . . . . . . .

**Sugar** is a general name used for sweeteners and is a key ingredient in baked goods. There are numerous types from different sources. I like organic cane sugar because this type of sugar is grown without synthetic pesticides. Even if organic, this is still SUGAR and should be consumed in minimal amounts.

**Coconut Sugar** is harvested from the sap of the coconut plant, and has a coarse texture, dark brown color, and intense flavor. Coconut sugar can be used to replace brown sugar and I have found that less is needed to achieve the same sweetness.

**Powdered Sugar**, also know as confectioner's sugar, is finely ground sugar blended with starch. Organic powdered sugar contains tapioca starch. Non-organic brands contain cornstarch with GMO's.

**Honey** that is raw and organic contains numerous vitamins and minerals. Containing only single sugars, this makes for easier absorption and processing by the body. Small amounts are needed to add a delicate, natural sweetness to baked goods.

**Maple Syrup** is a natural, unrefined liquid sweetener. Always use pure grade B maple syrup. In most recipes, maple syrup can be used in place of honey. To maintain freshness, refrigerate after opening.

..................................................................................

**Butter** adds a delightful taste and texture to baked goods. I use grass-fed butter.

**Coconut Oil** is fat extracted from the meat of the coconut. Depending on the recipe, either the solid or liquid state is used. For highest quality, look for coconut oil labeled organic, virgin, cold-pressed, or refined.

**Olive Oil** is a great source of heart-healthy fat and is high in vitamin E and antioxidants. Cold-pressed extra virgin olive oil offers the best nutrition.

..................................................................................

**Eggs** provide excellent texture and taste to a bakery item. An egg's nutritional value is dependent on the chicken's diet and environment. For best results, purchase eggs from a local farmer that you know and trust.

..................................................................................

**Baking Powder** helps baked goods rise. I recommend using aluminum-free baking powder to avoid the unnecessary consumption of metals. Freshness is a critical factor in baking powder's performance, so purchase smaller containers in hopes of using the entire container before the expiration date.

**Baking Soda** also adds volume to a bakery items. Many recipes use a combination of baking soda and baking powder to achieve a perfect spring in the finished product. Freshness is critical to performance.

**Active Dry Yeast** is a leavening ingredient used in many bread and breakfast pastry recipes. Often considered too complicated to use, yeast delivers the necessary action to make a dough rise. When simple instructions are followed, results are amazing. Refrigerate to ensure freshness.

..................................................................................

**Dried Buttermilk** is a great substitution for the real thing. Use proportions on ingredient package as your guide. Simply add the buttermilk powder to the recipe's dry ingredients and add water to the recipe's liquid ingredients. This ingredient is best to keep in the refrigerator.

**Coconut Milk** is the puree of coconut meat and coconut water. Look for canned coconut milk that is free from guar gum and added sugar. Full-fat coconut milk provides the best flavor and nutrition.

. . . . . . . . . . . . . . . . . . . . . . . . . . . . . . . . . . . . . . . . . . . . . . . . . . . . . . . . . .

**Potato Flakes** are a convenient way to add potato flavor and starch to a recipe. Potato starch adds structure and texture to yeast breads and pastries. Make sure to use potato flakes and not potato buds.

**Tapioca Starch** is used as a thickening agent in recipes and comes from the root of the cassava, which is a woody shrub native to South America. Use tapioca starch to help bind ingredients together and create a smooth texture.

. . . . . . . . . . . . . . . . . . . . . . . . . . . . . . . . . . . . . . . . . . . . . . . . . . . . . . . . . .

**Salt** brightens the flavor of baked goods. Celtic and Himalayan salts are unbleached, unrefined and contain healthy minerals.

. . . . . . . . . . . . . . . . . . . . . . . . . . . . . . . . . . . . . . . . . . . . . . . . . . . . . . . . . .

**Chocolate Chips** are a sweet addition to baked goods and treats. Try to look for brands that are free of soy, dairy, and gluten. The higher the cacao percentage, the less sugar added.

**Cacao Nibs** are chopped cacao beans that contain no added sugars or fats. They have a crunchy texture and offer a burst of pure cacao flavor.

**Cocoa Powder** is made from cacao beans that have been roasted, ground, and freed from fatty oils. Look for brands with no added sugars.

. . . . . . . . . . . . . . . . . . . . . . . . . . . . . . . . . . . . . . . . . . . . . . . . . . . . . . . . . .

**Peanut Butter** adds flavor, texture, and nutrition to a baked item. Make sure to look for a label that reads organic pure peanut butter. Stir well before using and refrigerate after opening.

**Nuts and Seeds** are a good source of protein and add a great deal of variety, texture, and taste to recipes. Always look for nuts that are raw or dry roasted, without salt or oil. Keep nuts refrigerated to assure freshness.

**Dried Fruits** add sweetness to a recipe. Make sure to read ingredient statements and purchase fruits that have no added sugar.

**Freeze Dried Fruits** add fruit flavor and natural color to a recipe.

**Unsweetened Flaked Coconut** adds flavor and nutrition to a recipe. When pureed, unsweetened flaked coconut becomes a flour. Look for brands that are unsulfured and unsweetened. After opening, refrigerate coconut.

⋯⋯⋯⋯⋯⋯⋯⋯⋯⋯⋯⋯⋯⋯⋯⋯⋯⋯⋯⋯⋯⋯⋯⋯⋯⋯⋯⋯⋯⋯⋯⋯⋯⋯⋯⋯⋯⋯⋯⋯⋯⋯⋯

**Canned Beans** are a great way to add fiber and protein to a bakery item. I have incorporated black beans, northern beans, and chickpeas into some of the recipes in this book. Make sure to avoid brands that have added sugar and preservatives.

**Pumpkin Puree** is cooked or canned pumpkin. Be sure to use pumpkin puree not pumpkin pie filling. Pumpkin pie filling is sweetened and spiced.

⋯⋯⋯⋯⋯⋯⋯⋯⋯⋯⋯⋯⋯⋯⋯⋯⋯⋯⋯⋯⋯⋯⋯⋯⋯⋯⋯⋯⋯⋯⋯⋯⋯⋯⋯⋯⋯⋯⋯⋯⋯⋯⋯

**Tahini** is a paste made from sesame seeds, and is rich in minerals, protein, and healthy fat. Hummus recipes commonly use tahini. In a bakery item, tahini adds a sweet, nutty flavor. I like to buy tahini at an Asian grocery store.

⋯⋯⋯⋯⋯⋯⋯⋯⋯⋯⋯⋯⋯⋯⋯⋯⋯⋯⋯⋯⋯⋯⋯⋯⋯⋯⋯⋯⋯⋯⋯⋯⋯⋯⋯⋯⋯⋯⋯⋯⋯⋯⋯

**Flavorings** are used to make bakery taste amazing. Always use pure vanilla and almond extracts and use organic herbs and spices. The quality is worth the extra cost.

**Essential Oils** have concentrated pure flavor and are a great alternative to traditional flavorings. Be sure to use a quality brand that is therapeutic, certified organic, or wild-crafted.

⋯⋯⋯⋯⋯⋯⋯⋯⋯⋯⋯⋯⋯⋯⋯⋯⋯⋯⋯⋯⋯⋯⋯⋯⋯⋯⋯⋯⋯⋯⋯⋯⋯⋯⋯⋯⋯⋯⋯⋯⋯⋯⋯

**Protein Powder** adds a boost of protein to healthy snack recipes. Look for brands that are undenatured, naturally-sweetened, and organic.

## Tools and Equipment

There are almost as many kitchen tools and gadgets available today as there are ingredients! Collecting is easy while thinking they will serve a purpose; however, many are unnecessary. Take an inventory of the tools and equipment in your kitchen. Decide which ones you use the most; organize and keep them in an easily accessible area. Store the ones you infrequently use in another area or "pay it forward" by donating them to a thrift shop.

You can make baked goods with a minimal amount of tools and equipment. Here are a few items that I frequently use:

**Mixing Bowls:** Have 2 or 3 sizes of glass or metal bowls. Many recipes instruct you to mix dry ingredients in one bowl and liquid ingredients in another bowl before combining them together.

**Measuring Cups and Spoons:** Precise ingredient measurement is necessary when baking. You will need a standard set of measuring cups and a standard set of measuring spoons.

**Stand or Hand Mixer:** Electric mixers are convenient and don't require manual labor; however, an electric hand mixer takes up less space and will get the job done at a fraction of the cost.

**Food Processor:** This appliance will chop, grate, grind, and puree ingredients. Most models have a greater capacity then blenders; therefore, offer more versatility.

**Baking Sheets and Pans:** Higher-quality aluminum pans tend to give the best results. I recommend having: 2 to 3 baking sheets, a standard muffin tin with 2½-inch diameter cavities, a 7-inch bread pan, a 9-inch square or round cake pan, a 9x13-inch baking pan, and a 9-inch pie tin.

If you want to create baked goods with unique shape, I recommend investing in: a mini bundt pan, a donut pan, a whoopie pie pan, and mini loaf pans. Silicone baking molds are another great way to make cookies, protein bites, and chocolates visually appealing. I have enjoyed using specialty pans and silicone molds for some of the recipes in this cookbook.

**Parchment Paper:** Lining a baking sheet with parchment paper makes for an easy cleanup. Covering the bottom of a cake or loaf pan with a piece ensures your breads and cakes will easily fall out of the pan. Rolling out dough between two pieces eliminates the need for extra flour.

# Cookies

Chocolate Chip Cookies ................................................................ 1

Oatmeal Raisin Cookies ................................................................ 2

Snickerdoodles ............................................................................ 3

Gingersnaps ................................................................................ 6

Double Chocolate Cookies ............................................................ 7

Peanut Butter Cookies ................................................................. 8

Snowballs .................................................................................... 9

Party Time Cookies .................................................................... 10

Sugar Cookie Cutouts ................................................................. 11

Powdered Sugar Icing ................................................................ 12

Cinnamon Bark Honey Bears ...................................................... 13

Natural Rainbow Sprinkles ......................................................... 15

# Chocolate Chip Cookies

**Yield: 24 cookies**

*A remake of the universally popular cookie. Every cookie lover's passion begins with the unbeatable "comfort" of eating a warm chocolate chip cookie. This was the first recipe I reformulated and the last one I tested over and over to get it just right!*

1 cup Einkorn flour
½ cup almond flour
½ teaspoon baking soda
½ teaspoon salt
6 tablespoons butter, softened
¼ cup coconut sugar
2 tablespoons sugar
1 egg, lightly beaten
1 teaspoon vanilla
¾ cup chocolate chips

- In a medium bowl, combine flours, baking soda and salt; set aside.
- In a large bowl, cream butter, sugars, egg and vanilla. Add dry ingredients; mix until just combined. Stir in chocolate chips. Let dough rest 10 minutes.
- Drop dough by rounded spoonfuls 1 inch apart onto parchment paper-lined baking sheets. Flatten slightly with damp hand into ½-inch thick disks.
- Bake at 375° for 12-15 minutes or until lightly browned. Cool for 5 minutes before removing to wire racks to cool completely.

# Oatmeal Raisin Cookies

**Yield: 24 cookies**

A high-energy, healthy lunch box treat. Classmates and coworkers will be envious of this homemade chewy dessert.

**Tip:**
To enhance flavor, add 2-3 drops cinnamon bark and 1 drop nutmeg essential oils to the dough.

**Variations:**
Prepare as described except substitute goji berries, dried cranberries, chocolate chips or white chocolate chips for the raisins.

½ cup Einkorn flour
3 tablespoons flaxseed meal
½ teaspoon baking soda
½ teaspoon salt
½ teaspoon cinnamon
¼ teaspoon nutmeg
6 tablespoons butter, softened
1/3 cup coconut sugar
1 egg, lightly beaten
1 teaspoon vanilla
1 cup old-fashioned oats
1 cup raisins

- In a small bowl, combine flour, flaxseed meal, baking soda, salt and spices: set aside.
- In a large bowl, cream butter, coconut sugar. Add egg and vanilla; mix well. Add dry ingredients; blend until combined. Stir in oats and raisins. Let dough rest 10 minutes.
- Drop dough by rounded spoonfuls 1 inch apart onto parchment paper-lined baking sheets. Flatten slightly with damp hand into ½-inch thick disks.
- Bake at 350° for 12-15 minutes or until lightly browned. Cool for 5 minutes before removing to wire racks to cool completely.

# Snickerdoodles

**Yield: 24 cookies**

*A chewy, homespun snickerdoodle was my grandma's favorite coffee-dunking cookie. We always wondered where the name came from.*

1 cup Einkorn flour

½ cup almond flour

½ teaspoon baking soda

1 teaspoon cream of tartar

¼ teaspoon salt

¼ cup olive oil

⅓ cup sugar plus 2 tablespoons for coating

1 egg, lightly beaten

1 teaspoon vanilla

2 teaspoons cinnamon for coating

- In a medium bowl, combine flours, baking soda, cream of tartar and salt; set aside.
- In a large bowl, whisk olive oil and ⅓ cup sugar. Add egg and vanilla; mix well. Add dry ingredients; blend until just combined. Let dough rest 10 minutes.
- Blend 2 tablespoons sugar and 2 teaspoons cinnamon in a shallow dish. Drop dough by rounded spoonfuls into cinnamon-sugar mixture; roll to coat. Place 2 inches apart on parchment paper-lined baking sheets.
- Bake at 400° for 10-12 minutes or until lightly browned. Cool for 10 minutes before removing to wire racks to cool completely.

Gingersnaps p6    Double Chocolate p7

Chocolate Chip p1

Party Time p10

Oatmeal Raisin p2    Snowballs p9

Sugar Cookie Cutouts  p11

Cinnamon Bark Honey Bears  p13

Snickerdoodles  p3
Peanut Butter  p8

Natural Rainbow Sprinkles  p15

# Gingersnaps

**Yield: 24 cookies**

Ginger, cloves, nutmeg, cinnamon, and molasses create an unforgettable aroma while baking. Memories of special times flash before me when I smell and taste these crackled morsels!

**Tip:**
To enhance flavor, add 2-3 drops ginger, 2-3 drops cinnamon bark, 1-2 drops cloves and 1 drop nutmeg essential oils to the dough.

1 cup Einkorn flour
½ cup almond flour
1 teaspoon baking soda
¼ teaspoon salt
½ teaspoon ginger
½ teaspoon cinnamon
¼ teaspoon nutmeg
¼ teaspoon cloves
¼ cup butter, melted and cooled
2 tablespoons sugar plus 2 tablespoons for coating
¼ cup coconut sugar
2 tablespoons molasses
1 egg, lightly beaten

- In a medium bowl, combine flours, baking soda, salt and spices; set aside.
- In a large bowl, whisk melted butter, 2 tablespoons sugar, coconut sugar and molasses. Add egg; mix well. Add dry ingredients; blend until just combined. Let dough rest 10 minutes.
- Place 2 tablespoons sugar in a shallow dish. Drop dough by rounded spoonfuls into sugar; roll to coat. Place 2 inches apart on parchment paper-lined baking sheets.
- Bake at 350° for 10-12 minutes or until lightly browned. Cool for 5 minutes before removing to wire racks to cool completely.

# Double Chocolate Cookies

**Yield: 24 cookies**

*Just one bite and chocolate lovers will melt over these decadent brownie-like cookies. Dress them up by dusting with powdered sugar or garnishing with whole pecans or chocolate chips.*

4 ounces bittersweet chocolate (60-70% cacao)
1 tablespoon butter
2 tablespoon Einkorn flour
¼ teaspoon baking powder
¼ teaspoon salt
1 egg, lightly beaten
2 tablespoons honey
¼ cup coconut sugar
½ teaspoon vanilla
¼ cup chocolate chips plus more for garnish (optional)
whole pecans (optional)
powdered sugar (optional)

- In a small bowl, microwave chocolate and butter until melted; set aside and let cool.
- In another small bowl, combine flour, baking powder and salt; set aside.
- In a large bowl, blend egg, honey, coconut sugar and vanilla. Add melted chocolate mixture; mix well. Add dry ingredients; mix until just combined. Stir in chocolate chips. Let batter rest 10 minutes.
- Drop batter by rounded spoonfuls 2 inches apart onto parchment paper-lined baking sheets.
- Bake at 350° for 10-12 minutes or until edges are firm. Immediately press a whole pecan or chocolate chips in center of each cookie or lightly dust with powdered sugar. Cool for 10 minutes before removing to wire racks to cool completely.

# Peanut Butter Cookies

**Yield: 36 cookies**

*"Pure pleasure" describes the joy of dunking this old-fashioned cookie into a glass of milk! Emboss with a traditional crisscross, bake in a fun-shaped silicone baking mold, or decorate with chocolate chips.*

1 cup Einkorn flour
½ cup almond flour
½ teaspoon baking soda
½ teaspoon salt
6 tablespoons butter, softened
½ cup organic, no-sugar-added peanut butter
½ cup coconut sugar
1 egg, lightly beaten
2 teaspoons vanilla
2½ tablespoons sugar for coating
chocolate chips (optional)

- In a medium bowl, combine flours, baking soda and salt; set aside.

- In a large bowl, cream butter, peanut butter and coconut sugar. Add egg and vanilla; mix well. Add dry ingredients; mix until just combined. Let dough rest 10 minutes.

- Place sugar in a shallow dish. Drop dough by rounded spoonfuls into sugar; roll to coat. Place 1 inch apart on parchment paper-lined baking sheets or in silicone baking mold. If desired, flatten by making crisscross marks with tines of a fork.

- Bake at 350° for 10-12 minutes or until edges are firm and bottoms are lightly browned. Immediately press chocolate chip in center of each cookie (optional). Cool for 5 minutes before removing to wire racks to cool completely.

# Snowballs

**Yield: 30 cookies**

*Several other names have been given to this cookie: Russian Tea Cakes, Almond Crescents, or Wedding Tea Cakes. Regardless the name, they simply melt in your mouth.*

**Tip:**
Let Snowballs cool for at least 30 minutes before plating or storing. These cookies can be quite fragile until they have cooled completely.

1 cup Einkorn flour
1 cup almond flour
1 cup sliced almonds, coarsely ground
½ cup butter, softened
¼ cup sugar
1 teaspoon almond extract
3 tablespoons powdered sugar for coating

- In a medium bowl, combine flours and ground almonds; set aside.
- In large bowl, cream butter, sugar and almond extract. Add dry ingredients; blend until combined. Let dough rest 10 minutes.
- Drop dough by rounded spoonfuls 1 inch apart onto parchment paper-lined baking sheets.
- Bake at 350° for 12-15 minutes or until bottoms are lightly browned. Cool for 5 minutes.
- Place powdered sugar in shallow dish. While cookies are still warm, gently roll in powdered sugar to coat. Cool completely on wire racks.

# Party Time Cookies

**Yield: 30 cookies**

*Loaded with chunks of chocolate and almonds, the dough may seem crumbly. Once baked, the honey, butter, and flour "glue" the dough together. The end result . . . a heavenly bite of goodness!*

½ cup Einkorn flour
½ cup almond flour
1 cup chocolate chips
1 cup sliced almonds
¼ cup butter, softened
3 tablespoons honey
1 teaspoon vanilla
¼ teaspoon almond extract

- In a medium bowl, combine flours, chocolate chips and almonds; set aside.
- In large bowl, cream butter, honey, vanilla and almond extract. Add dry ingredients; blend until well combined. Let dough rest 10 minutes.
- Drop dough by rounded spoonfuls 1 inch apart onto parchment paper-lined baking sheets. Flatten slightly with damp hand into ½-inch thick disks.
- Bake at 350° for 12-15 minutes or until lightly browned. Cool for 10 minutes before removing to wire racks to cool completely.

# Sugar Cookie Cutouts

**Yield: 30 cookies**

*Cutouts were one of the most popular cookies at my shop. Customers and family members alike have fond memories associated with these decorative, sweet treats; therefore, I needed to get this recipe just right. Despite new flours and less sugar, the integrity of this cookie has been maintained!*

1 cup Einkorn flour
½ cup almond flour
½ teaspoon salt
¼ teaspoon baking soda
¼ teaspoon baking powder
¼ cup butter, softened
⅓ cup sugar
2 tablespoons sour cream
1 teaspoon vanilla
1 recipe Powdered Sugar Icing, page 12 (optional)
1 recipe Natural Rainbow Sprinkles, page 15 (optional)

- In a medium bowl, combine flours, salt, baking soda and baking powder; set aside.
- In large bowl, cream butter, sugar, sour cream and vanilla. Add dry ingredients; blend until well combined. Let dough rest 15 minutes.
- On a lightly floured piece of parchment paper, place half of the dough. Lightly flour top of dough; cover with another piece of parchment paper. Roll dough to ⅛ inch thick; remove top piece of parchment paper. Cut dough with 3-inch cookie cutter. Gently lift cutout dough and place 1 inch apart onto parchment paper-lined baking sheets. Repeat with remaining dough.
- Bake at 350° for 10-12 minutes or until lightly browned. Cool for 10 minutes before removing to wire racks to cool completely. If desired, frost with Powdered Sugar Icing and decorate with Natural Rainbow Sprinkles.

# Powdered Sugar Icing

**Yield: 30 cookies**

*An easy recipe that can be used to enhance many baked goods. The consistency can be customized based on your application. Simply add a dash of powdered sugar to thicken or a splash of hot water to thin.*

2 tablespoons butter

2 teaspoons water

⅔ cup powdered sugar

¼ teaspoon almond extract

- In a medium bowl, microwave butter and water until butter is melted.
- Add powdered sugar and almond extract; blend until well combined.

# Cinnamon Bark Honey Bears

**Yield: 15 cookies**

*Watching a child's face light up when they bite into this cookie and knowing that they are enjoying something that's good for them, makes the labor required for these cookies worthwhile.*

**Tip:**
To prevent sticking when chopping dates, spray your knife or kitchen shears with cooking spray.

1 cup Einkorn flour
1 cup almond flour
¼ teaspoon baking powder
1 teaspoon cinnamon
1 teaspoon ginger
½ teaspoon nutmeg
¼ teaspoon allspice
4 dates, chopped finely
¼ cup coconut oil, melted and cooled
3 tablespoon maple syrup
1 egg, lightly beaten
1 teaspoon vanilla
4 drops cinnamon bark essential oil
30 goji berries
½ recipe Powdered Sugar Icing, page 12 (optional)

- In a medium bowl, combine flours, baking powder, spices and chopped dates; set aside.
- In large bowl, whisk melted coconut oil and maple syrup. Add egg and vanilla; mix well. Add dry ingredients; blend until well combined. With hands, knead essential oil into dough. Let dough rest 15 minutes.

# Cinnamon Bark Honey Bears cont.

- On a lightly floured piece of parchment paper, place half of the dough. Lightly flour top of dough; cover with another piece of parchment paper. Roll dough to 1/4 inch thick; remove top piece of parchment paper. Cut dough with 3-inch bear-shaped cookie cutter. Gently lift cutout dough and place 1 inch apart onto parchment paper-lined baking sheets. Repeat with remaining dough.

- Use dough scraps to make bear faces. Make one small ball for muzzle and 3 smaller balls for eyes and nose; gently press into cutout dough. Use goji berries to make bow ties. Cut one widthwise for bow and one lengthwise for ties; gently press into cutout dough.

- Bake at 350° for 12-15 minutes or until lightly brown. Remove from oven. Lower oven temperature to 200°; bake an additional 5-10 minutes until cookies are crisp. Cool for 10 minutes before removing to wire racks to cool completely. If desired, pipe ears and paws with Powdered Sugar Icing.

# Natural Rainbow Sprinkles

**Yield: ¼ cup**

*Vegetables and spices provide the beautiful color for these naturally-sweetened sprinkles! They add a fun spark of color to cookies, cakes, donuts, and more!*

**Tip:**
Grind the vegetable first and then measure for this recipe. A food processor works best to finely grind the raw vegetables. Cut vegetable into small pieces, place in food processor and pulse until small, uniform pieces are achieved.

**Tip:**
White sprinkles can be made by simply pulsing ¼ cup unsweetened flaked coconut in a food processor. If a sweeter taste is desired, add ½ teaspoon of powdered stevia. Dehydrating in the oven is not necessary.

¼ cup unsweetened flaked coconut
½ teaspoon powdered stevia
Plus, **one** of the following:
   For RED, 4 teaspoons finely ground peeled raw beet
   For ORANGE, 4 teaspoons finely ground peeled raw carrot
   For GREEN, 4 teaspoons finely ground raw spinach
   For YELLOW, ½ teaspoon ground turmeric

- **In food processor, add coconut, stevia and ground vegetable or spice; pulse until well blended and pieces are uniformly sized.**
- **Spread in thin layer on a foil-lined baking sheet.**
- **Dehydrate in 170° oven for 45 minutes, stirring every 15 minutes. Cool completely. Store in an airtight container; refrigerate up to 2 months or freeze up to 6 months.**

# Breads & Pastries

Banana Bread ..................................................................... 19

Zucchini Bread .................................................................. 20

Pumpkin Bread ................................................................. 21

Morning Glory Muffins ..................................................... 24

Muffins ............................................................................... 25

Donuts ............................................................................... 27

Glazes ................................................................................ 28

Breakfast Scones .............................................................. 29

Classic Wheat Bread ........................................................ 31

Multigrain Einkorn Bread ................................................ 33

Cinnamon Rolls ................................................................ 35

Cinnamon Roll Frosting .................................................. 37

# Banana Bread

**Yield: 7-inch loaf**

*My grandsons will purposely not eat a couple of bananas from a bunch. They do this in hopes that their mom will bake the overripe bananas into this delicious bread!*

**Tip:**
Any size loaf pan can be used. Fill pans two-thirds full. If you have extra batter, use it to make muffins.

**Tip:**
Ripe bananas can be placed in an airtight container and stored in the freezer. Simply defrost for about 10 minutes before mashing and incorporating into recipe.

1 cup Einkorn flour
½ teaspoon baking soda
½ teaspoon baking powder
½ teaspoon salt
1 cup mashed ripe bananas (2 medium)
2 tablespoons sour cream
¼ cup butter or coconut oil, melted and cooled
2 tablespoons honey
¼ cup coconut sugar
1 egg, lightly beaten
1 teaspoon vanilla
½ cup chocolate chips or nuts (optional)

- In a medium bowl, combine flour, baking soda, baking powder and salt; set aside.
- In another medium bowl, whisk mashed banana and sour cream; set aside.
- In a large bowl, whisk melted butter or coconut oil, honey, coconut sugar, egg and vanilla. Add dry ingredients; stir until just combined. Fold in banana mixture. Fold in chocolate chips and/or nuts (optional).
- Spoon batter into a greased pan. Let batter rest 10 minutes.
- Bake at 350° for 20-30 minutes or until toothpick inserted near center comes out clean. Cool in pan on wire rack for 10 minutes. Remove loaf from pan; cool completely before slicing.

# Zucchini Bread

**Yield: 7-inch loaf**

*Perfect for breakfast or an after school snack. A whole loaf eaten by one person? It has happened more than once in my house!*

**Variation:
Apple Bread**
Substitute 1 cup shredded apple for shredded zucchini and substitute ½ cup applesauce for mashed ripe banana.

1 cup shredded zucchini
1 cup Einkorn flour
½ teaspoon baking soda
½ teaspoon baking powder
½ teaspoon salt
1 teaspoon cinnamon
1 teaspoon allspice
¼ cup butter or coconut oil, melted and cooled
2 tablespoons honey
¼ cup coconut sugar
1 egg, lightly beaten
½ tablespoon fresh lemon juice
½ cup mashed ripe banana (1 medium)
2 tablespoons sour cream
½ cup nuts (optional)

- Shred zucchini and squeeze between several layers of paper towel to remove excess moisture.
- In a medium bowl, combine flour, baking soda, baking powder, salt and spices; set aside.
- In a large bowl, whisk melted butter or coconut oil, honey, coconut sugar, egg, lemon juice, mashed banana and sour cream. Add dry ingredients; stir until just combined. Fold in zucchini. Fold in nuts (optional).
- Spoon batter into a greased pan. Let batter rest 10 minutes.
- Bake at 350° for 20-30 minutes or until toothpick inserted near center comes out clean. Cool in pan on wire rack for 10 minutes. Remove loaf from pan; cool completely before slicing.

# Pumpkin Bread

**Yield: 7-inch loaf**

*Often thought of as an autumnal ingredient, pumpkin puree is commonly used in fall and winter baking. Not only does pumpkin lend itself to sweet applications, but is packed with nutrition–fiber, vitamin A and iron, and can serve as a fat substitute. For these reasons, one should be inspired to make pumpkin bread any time of year.*

1 cup Einkorn flour
¼ cup old-fashioned oats, finely ground
1 teaspoon baking soda
½ teaspoon salt
1½ teaspoons cinnamon
1 teaspoon ginger
½ teaspoon nutmeg
¼ teaspoon cloves
¼ cup butter or coconut oil, melted and cooled
¼ cup maple syrup
1 cup pumpkin puree
3 eggs, lightly beaten
1 teaspoon vanilla

- In a medium bowl, combine flour, ground oats, baking soda, salt and spices; set aside.
- In a large bowl, whisk melted butter or coconut oil, maple syrup, pumpkin puree, eggs and vanilla. Add dry ingredients; stir until just combined.
- Spoon batter into a greased pan. Let batter rest 10 minutes.
- Bake at 350° for 20-30 minutes or until toothpick inserted near center comes out clean. Cool in pan on wire rack for 10 minutes. Remove loaf from pan; cool completely before slicing.

Pumpkin Bread  p21

Banana Bread  p19

Zucchini Bread  p20

Morning Glory Muffins  p24

Classic Wheat Bread  p31

Donuts  p27

Breakfast Scones  p29

Muffins  p25

Multigrain Einkorn Bread  p33

Cinnamon Rolls  p35

# Morning Glory Muffins

**Yield: 20 muffins**

*Apple, maple syrup, and applesauce replace ingredients found in the traditional recipe. This is a hearty, moist muffin packed with flavorful spices and tidbits of nuts, fruit, and carrot.*

**Tip:**
Muffin cups of all shapes and sizes can be used. Adjust the baking time according to the pan you use. Mini muffins will bake about 8 minutes faster than standard size muffins. Yield for mini muffins will vary.

⅓ cup coconut oil, melted and cooled
¼ cup maple syrup
⅓ cup applesauce
3 eggs, lightly beaten
1 teaspoon vanilla
1 cup Einkorn flour
1 cup old-fashioned oats, finely ground
2 teaspoons baking soda
½ teaspoon salt
2 teaspoons cinnamon
1 cup grated carrot
1 cup grated apple
½ cup unsweetened flaked coconut
½ cup raisins
½ cup chopped walnuts

- In medium bowl, whisk melted coconut oil, maple syrup, applesauce, eggs and vanilla; set aside.
- In a large bowl, combine flour, ground oats, baking soda, salt and cinnamon. Add grated carrot, grated apple, coconut, raisins and walnuts; blend. Add wet ingredients; stir until just combined.
- Spoon batter into greased or paper-lined 2½-inch muffin cups, filling two-thirds full. Let batter rest for 10 minutes
- Bake at 350° for 15-20 minutes or until toothpick inserted near center comes out clean. Cool muffins in pan on wire rack for 5 minutes. Remove muffins from pan; serve warm or room temperature.

# *Muffins*

Yield: 12 muffins

*Every morning, my shop's door opened with over 12 varieties of fresh, warm muffins. We started with a basic batter and added many ingredients which made our muffins into something similar to a cupcake. Now that I have become aware that many other bakeries have done this same thing, I am delighted to share this healthier version.*

2 cups Einkorn flour
⅓ cup coconut sugar
2 teaspoons baking powder
½ teaspoon baking soda
1 teaspoon salt
¼ cup butter or coconut oil, melted
1 cup buttermilk
1 egg, lightly beaten
1 teaspoon vanilla

- In a medium bowl, combine flour, coconut sugar, baking powder, baking soda and salt; set aside.
- In a large bowl, whisk melted butter or coconut oil, buttermilk, egg and vanilla. Add dry ingredients; stir until just combined.
- Spoon batter into greased or paper-lined 2½-inch muffin cups, filling two-thirds full. Let batter rest 10 minutes.
- Bake at 375° for 15-20 minutes or until toothpick inserted near center comes out clean. Cool muffins in pan on wire rack for 5 minutes. Remove muffins from pan; serve warm or room temperature.

# Muffins cont.

## Muffin Variations

**Tip:**
Buttermilk can be substituted with acidified milk. Place ½ tablespoon lemon juice in a liquid measuring cup. Add milk to bring liquid up to the 1-cup measuring line; let sit for 10 minutes. Milk will look curdled.

**Lemon Blueberry Muffins**
Fold 1 cup fresh or frozen blueberries coated in 1 tablespoon flour and add 2-4 drops lemon essential oil into batter.

**Chocolate Chip Muffins**
Fold 1 cup chocolate chips into batter.

**Fruit & Nut Muffins**
Fold ½ cup raisins, snipped dried apricots, or snipped dried apples and ½ cup walnuts or pecans into batter.

**Multigrain Muffins**
Substitute 1 cup old-fashioned oats, finely ground in place of one of the cups of Einkorn flour.

# Donuts

**Yield: 18 mini donuts or 12 large donuts**

*My customers would often ask why we did not offer donuts. Most bakeshops fry them and that never appealed to me. This baked version is a much healthier way to offer this breakfast favorite on your menu. On Christmas morning, my grandsons decorated these bakery gems for our holiday breakfast. "Better than the donut shop's," they told me. What a compliment!*

1 cup Einkorn flour
1 tablespoon tapioca starch
1¼ teaspoon baking powder
¾ teaspoon salt
2 tablespoons butter or coconut oil, melted and cooled
2 tablespoons honey
½ cup buttermilk
1 egg, lightly beaten
1 teaspoon vanilla
1 recipe White Glaze, page 28 (optional)
1 recipe Chocolate Glaze, page 28 (optional)
½ recipe Natural Rainbow Sprinkles, page 15 (optional)

- In a medium bowl, combine flour, tapioca starch, baking powder and salt; set aside.
- In a large bowl, whisk melted butter or coconut oil, honey, buttermilk, egg and vanilla. Add dry ingredients; stir until just combined.
- Spoon batter into greased donut pan. Let batter rest 10 minutes.
- Bake at 425° for 4-6 minutes. Cool in pan on wire rack for 5 minutes before removing. If desired, dip donut tops in White or Chocolate Glaze and decorate with Natural Rainbow Sprinkles.

Donut variations on page 28.

# Glazes

**Variation:
Chocolate Donuts**
Add ¼ cup cocoa powder to the dry ingredient mixture.

**Variation:
Spiced Donuts**
Add ½ teaspoon apple pie spice to the dry ingredient mixture.

## White Glaze

1 tablespoon butter

1 teaspoon water

¼ cup powdered sugar

1 drop almond extract

- In a medium bowl, microwave butter and water until butter is melted.
- Add powdered sugar and almond extract; blend until well combined.

## Chocolate Glaze

1 tablespoon butter

1 teaspoon water

¼ cup chocolate chips

- In a medium bowl, microwave butter and water until butter is melted.
- Add chocolate chips; stir until melted into butter mixture.

# Breakfast Scones

**Yield: 8-12 scones**

*Scones have become a staple in many coffee shops. Like many bakery items, the recipes have been loaded with so many ingredients that the simple taste and texture have been lost. I think the use of both Einkorn flour and oat flour in my recipe makes it a winner. The final product is slightly sweet with a tender bite.*

**Tip:**
Customize the flavor of your scones by adding 4-6 drops of your favorite essential oil. Add essential oil with buttermilk.

1 cup Einkorn flour
1 cup old-fashioned oats, finely ground
1 tablespoon baking powder
2 tablespoons sugar
½ teaspoon salt
6 tablespoons cold butter, cut into small cubes
½ cup buttermilk

1 egg, lightly beaten
1 tablespoon old-fashioned oats

- In a large bowl, combine flour, ground oats, baking powder, sugar and salt. Using pastry blender or fingers, cut in butter until mixture resembles coarse crumbs. Add buttermilk; stir until large clumps form. With hands, gently knead dough just until dry ingredients are absorbed.

- Turn dough out onto lightly floured surface; gently pat into a 7-inch circle about 1 inch thick. Cut into 8 large or 12 small wedges; place on parchment paper-lined baking sheet 2 inches apart. Brush tops of wedges with beaten egg; sprinkle with oats.

- Bake at 425° for 15-18 minutes or until golden. Cool for 5 minutes before removing to wire racks to cool completely.

# Breakfast Scones cont.

**Scone Variations**

**Goji Berry Scones**
Hydrate ½ cup goji berries in ¼ cup boiling water for 5 minutes; drain excess water. Toss hydrated goji berries in 1 tablespoon of flour; add to the dry ingredients.

**Chocolate Chip Scones**
Add ½ cup chocolate chips to the dry ingredients.

# Classic Wheat Bread

**Yield: 8-inch loaf**

*Bread has become filled with so many altered ingredients that the authentic "staff-of-life" taste and texture have been lost. Determined not to add modern ingredients to this bread, I found myself going back to my grandma's recipe that used basic ingredients and simple techniques. She always used her leftover mashed potatoes and the water she boiled them in. My heart was warmed when I met success using Einkorn flour in her original recipe.*

¼ cup warm water

1½ teaspoons active dry yeast

1 teaspoon sugar

- In a small bowl, combine water, yeast and sugar; let rest at room temperature for 10 minutes. Mixture will become bubbly and frothy.

1½ cup Einkorn flour

3 tablespoons mashed potato flakes

1 teaspoon salt

1 tablespoon sugar

1 cup warm water

yeast mixture (from above)

- In a large bowl, combine flour, potato flakes, salt, sugar, water and yeast mixture; stir until combined. Mixture will have spongy appearance. Cover bowl with plastic wrap; let rest at room temperature for 15 minutes.

1½ tablespoons coconut oil, melted and cooled

1 cup Einkorn flour

- To the spongy dough, add melted coconut oil and additional flour; stir until combined. Dough will be very sticky. Cover bowl again with plastic wrap; let rest at room temperature for 45 minutes.

# Classic Wheat Bread cont.

¹/₃ - ½ cup Einkorn flour

- Stir the dough, pulling it together. Add additional flour; stir until combined. Turn dough out onto a lightly floured surface; gently knead until soft, smooth dough forms. If necessary, add additional flour, 1 tablespoon at a time, until dough no longer sticks to your hands.

- Gently pat and pull dough into loaf shape; place in greased 8-inch loaf pan. Cover with clean, dry cloth; let rise in warm place until dough reaches top edge of loaf pan (30-50 minutes).

- Preheat oven to 425°. Place loaf pan in oven; lower oven temperature to 375°. Bake for 25-30 minutes or until bread sounds hollow when tapped with finger. Cool in pan on wire rack for 10 minutes. Remove loaf from pan; cool 2 hours on rack before slicing.

# Multigrain Einkorn Bread

Yield: 8-inch loaf

*This recipe was tucked away in my grandma's collection of family favorites. I use both Einkorn flour and oat flour in this recipe, resulting in a true multigrain bread. I am delighted with its taste, texture and nutrition. This bread is especially good toasted!*

¼ cup warm water
1½ teaspoons active dry yeast
1 teaspoon sugar

- In a small bowl, combine water, yeast and sugar; let rest at room temperature for 10 minutes. Mixture will become bubbly and frothy.

1½ cup Einkorn flour
3 tablespoons mashed potato flakes
1 teaspoon salt
¼ teaspoon cinnamon
1 tablespoon flax seeds
2 tablespoons sunflower seeds
1 cup warm water
yeast mixture (from above)

- In a large bowl, combine flour, potato flakes, salt, cinnamon, seeds, water and yeast mixture; stir until combined. Mixture will have spongy appearance. Cover with plastic wrap and let rest for 15 minutes.

1½ tablespoons coconut oil, melted and cooled
2 tablespoons honey
½ cup Einkorn flour
½ cup old-fashioned oats, finely ground

- To the spongy dough, add melted coconut oil, honey, flour and ground oats; stir until combined. Dough

# Multigrain Einkorn Bread cont.

will be very sticky. Cover bowl with plastic wrap; let rest at room temperature for 45 minutes.

½ - ⅔ cup Einkorn flour

- Stir the dough, pulling it together. Add additional flour; stir until combined. Turn dough out onto a lightly floured surface; gently knead until soft, smooth dough forms. If necessary, add 1 tablespoon at a time, until dough is no longer sticky.

1 egg, slightly beaten

1 teaspoon flax seeds

2 teaspoon sunflower seeds

- Gently pat and pull dough into loaf shape; place in greased 8-inch loaf pan. Brush top of loaf with beaten egg; sprinkle with flax and sunflower seeds. Cover with clean, dry cloth; let rise in warm place until dough reaches top edge of loaf pan (30-50 minutes).

- Preheat oven to 425°. Place loaf pan in oven; lower oven temperature to 375°. Bake for 25-30 minutes or until bread sounds hollow when tapped with finger. Cool in pan on wire rack for 10 minutes. Remove loaf from pan; cool 2 hours on rack before slicing.

# Cinnamon Rolls

**Yield: 12 rolls**

*Cinnamon rolls are my family's signature pastry. I have great memories of the time I spent in Grandma's kitchen learning how to make them. For this reason, I used the cinnamon roll to launch my bakery business. Now combining Einkorn flour with Grandma's techniques, I present a "better-for-you" version.*

¼ cup warm water
1½ teaspoons active dry yeast
1 teaspoon sugar

- In a small bowl, combine water, yeast and sugar; let rest at room temperature for 10 minutes. Mixture will become bubbly and frothy.

1½ cups Einkorn flour
3 tablespoons mashed potato flakes
2 tablespoons dry milk or buttermilk powder
¾ teaspoon salt
½ teaspoon baking powder
3 tablespoons sugar
1 egg, slightly beaten
1 teaspoon vanilla
½ cup warm water
yeast mixture (from above)

- In a large bowl, combine flour, potato flakes, dry milk, salt, baking powder, sugar, egg, vanilla, water and yeast mixture; stir until combined. Mixture will have spongy appearance. Cover with plastic wrap and let rest for 15 minutes.

3 tablespoons coconut oil, melted and cooled
1 cup Einkorn flour

- To the spongy dough, add melted coconut oil and additional flour; stir until combined. Dough will be very sticky. Cover bowl with plastic wrap; let rest at room temperature for 45 minutes.

# Cinnamon Rolls cont.

**Tip:**
Cinnamon rolls can be made ahead and baked fresh the next morning. Prepare recipe through rolling stage; cover panned roll slices with plastic wrap and refrigerate overnight. In the morning, let rise and bake according to recipe directions.

4 to 6 tablespoons Einkorn flour

- Stir the dough, pulling it together. Add additional 2 tablespoons Einkorn flour; stir until combined. Turn dough out onto a floured surface; gently knead until soft, smooth dough forms. If necessary, add additional flour, 1 tablespoon at a time until dough no longer sticks to your hands. Let dough rest 10 minutes.

For the filling:

3 tablespoons sugar

2 tablespoons coconut sugar

1 ½ teaspoons cinnamon

1 teaspoon Einkorn flour

3 tablespoons butter, melted

- In a medium bowl, combine sugar, coconut sugar, cinnamon and flour. Add melted butter; stir until well blended.

- Place dough on generously floured cutting board; roll into 14x10-inch rectangle. Spread filling over dough. Roll up, jelly-roll style, starting from long side. Slice roll into 12 equal pieces. Place slices in parchment-paper lined 9x13-inch baking dish. Let rise in a warm place until nearly double in size (30-50 minutes).

- Bake at 375° for 20-22 minutes or until golden. Cool in pan on wire for 5 minutes. Drizzle with Cinnamon Roll Icing. (page 37).

# Cinnamon Roll Icing

Yield: 12 rolls

½ cup powdered sugar
1 - 1½ teaspoon warm water
1 drop almond extract (optional)
1-2 drops Orange essential oil (optional)

- In a small bowl, add powdered sugar, water and extract or essential oil (optional); stir until well blended.

# Pies & Tarts

Blueberry Galette ............................................................. 41

Pumpkin Pie ..................................................................... 45

Apple Crumb Pie .............................................................. 47

Classic Apple Pie .............................................................. 49

Banana Cream Tart .......................................................... 51

# Blueberry Galette

**Yield: 9-inch galette**

*A galette is a free-form rustic pie which offers all the flavor of a traditional pie, with a crisp buttery crust and sweet bubbly fruit filling, but without the fuss of panning and fluting a crust. Try replacing some of the blueberries with raspberries, juicy peaches, or plums.*

For the crust:

2 cups Einkorn flour

2 tablespoons sugar

½ teaspoon salt

7 tablespoons cold butter, cut into ¼-inch cubes

4 to 6 tablespoons ice water

- In a medium bowl, combine flour, sugar and salt. Using pastry blender or fingers, cut in butter until mixture resembles coarse crumbs. Sprinkle 4 tablespoons of water over the mixture; stir and press until dough holds together. If necessary, add additional water, 1 tablespoon at a time. Let dough rest 10 minutes.
- On a piece of parchment paper, use your hands to slightly flatten dough into a 4-inch disk. Roll dough from center to edges into a 13-inch circle. Leave dough on parchment paper; slide onto baking sheet.

# Blueberry Galette cont.

**Filling**

For the filling:
2 cups fresh or frozen blueberries
¼ cup sugar
1 tablespoon Einkorn flour
⅛ teaspoon salt
2 to 3 drops lemon essential oil (optional)

- In a medium bowl, combine blueberries, sugar, flour, salt and essential oil (optional). Place fruit mixture in center of dough, leaving a 2½-inch border. Fold border up over the blueberries; pleat dough to fit snuggly around fruit (refer to photo on page 43).

To finish the crust:
1 egg white, lightly beaten
1 teaspoon sugar

- Brush top of dough with egg white; sprinkle with 1 teaspoon sugar.
- Bake at 375° for 50-55 minutes or until crust is lightly brown and crisp and fruit mixture is bubbling. Cool 30 minutes before serving.

Blueberry Galette  p41

Pumpkin Pie  p45

Banana Cream Tart  p51

# Pumpkin Pie

Yield: 9-inch pie

*A traditional Thanksgiving dessert made with low-gluten Einkorn flour and less sugar. Serve with a dollop of freshly whipped cream and it will be the highlight of your next holiday gathering.*

**Tip:**
If crust begins to brown too quickly, cover with foil.

For the crust:

1½ cups Einkorn flour

½ teaspoon salt

6 tablespoons cold butter, cut into ¼-inch cubes

3 to 5 tablespoons ice water

- In a medium bowl, combine flour, sugar and salt. Using pastry blender or fingers, cut in butter until mixture resembles coarse crumbs. Sprinkle 3 tablespoons of water over the mixture; stir and press until dough holds together. If necessary, add additional water, 1 tablespoon at a time. Let dough rest 10 minutes.

- On floured surface, use hands to slightly flatten dough into a 4-inch disk. Roll dough from center to edges into a 12-inch circle. Loosely fold dough in half; gently lift and place onto 9-inch pie pan. Unfold dough and ease into pan. Trim dough to ½ inch beyond pan's edge. Tuck the overhanging dough under, even with pan's rim. Flute crust by placing thumb and index finger against the inside of the dough edge; press dough into the center of these fingers with other hand's index finger. Continue around entire edge of crust.

# Pumpkin Pie cont.

**Filling**

For the filling:

3 eggs, beaten

15 ounces (1¾ cups) pumpkin puree

⅓ cup coconut sugar

½ teaspoon salt

1 teaspoon cinnamon

½ teaspoon ginger

¼ teaspoon nutmeg

¼ teaspoon cloves

1 cup coconut milk or half-and-half

- In a large bowl, whisk eggs, pumpkin puree, coconut sugar, salt, spices and coconut milk or half-and-half until well blended. Pour into prepared crust.
- Bake at 425° for 15 minutes; lower oven to 350° and bake for additional 35-45 minutes or until filling is puffed and center wiggles slightly. Cool for 30 minutes before serving.

# Apple Crumb Pie

**Yield: 9-inch pie**

*A multigrain crumb topping differentiates this pie from the classic double-crust pie and is easier to make. Macintosh, Granny Smith, or Pippin apples have the perfect taste and texture for this recipe.*

For the crust:

1½ cups Einkorn flour

½ teaspoon salt

6 tablespoons cold butter, cut into ¼-inch cubes

3 to 5 tablespoons ice water

- In a medium bowl, combine flour and salt. Using pastry blender or fingers, cut in butter until mixture resembles coarse crumbs. Sprinkle 3 tablespoons of water over the mixture, stir and press until dough holds together. If necessary, add additional water, 1 tablespoon at a time. Let dough rest 10 minutes.
- On floured surface, use hands to slightly flatten dough into a 4-inch disk. Roll dough from center to edges into a 12-inch circle. Loosely fold dough in half; gently lift and place onto 9-inch pie pan. Unfold dough and ease into pan. Trim dough to ½ inch beyond pan's edge. Tuck the overhanging dough under, even with pan's rim. Flute crust by placing thumb and index finger against the inside of the dough edge; press dough into the center of these fingers with other hand's index finger. Continue around entire edge of crust.

# Apple Crumb Pie cont.

**Filling & Crumb Topping**

For the filling:

4 cups apples that are peeled, cored and sliced ¼-inch thick

⅓ cup coconut sugar

¼ cup Einkorn flour

1½ teaspoon cinnamon

¼ teaspoon nutmeg

- In a large bowl, combine apples, coconut sugar, flour and spices. Spread apple mixture in bottom of prepared crust.

For the crumb topping:

⅓ cup Einkorn flour

⅓ cup almond flour

⅓ cup old-fashioned oats, finely ground

¼ cup coconut sugar

6 tablespoons cold butter, cut into ¼-inch cubes

- In a large bowl, combine flours, ground oats and coconut sugar. Add butter; toss to coat. Pinch butter cubes between fingertips until mixture looks like crumbly wet sand. Distribute crumb topping evenly over apples.
- Bake at 400° for 15 minutes; lower oven to 350° and bake for additional 35-40 or until fruit is bubbling and crumb topping is a deep golden brown. Cool for 1 hour before serving.

# Classic Apple Pie

**Yield: 9-inch pie**

*Less sugar in the filling allows us to enjoy the natural sweetness of the fruit. For variety, the apples can be replaced with other fresh and frozen fruits.*

For the crust:

2¼ cups Einkorn flour

1 teaspoon salt

10 tablespoons cold butter, cut into ¼-inch cubes

5 to 7 tablespoons ice water

- In a medium bowl, combine flour and salt. Using pastry blender or fingers, cut in butter until mixture resembles coarse crumbs. Sprinkle 5 tablespoons of water over the mixture, stir and press until dough holds together. If necessary, add additional water, 1 tablespoon at a time. Divide dough into two even pieces; let dough rest 10 minutes.
- Use hands to slightly flatten each piece into a 4-inch disk. On a floured surface, roll one piece of dough from center to edges into a 12-inch circle. Loosely fold rolled dough in half; gently lift and place into 9-inch pie pan. Unfold dough and ease into pan.

For the filling:

4 cups apples that are peeled, cored and sliced ¼ inch thick

⅓ cup coconut sugar

¼ cup Einkorn flour

1½ teaspoon cinnamon

¼ teaspoon nutmeg

1 tablespoon butter, cut into ¼-inch cubes

# Classic Apple Pie cont.

**Variation:**
**Apple Cranberry Pie**
Substitute 1 cup fresh cranberries for 1 cup of the apples.

**Variation:**
**Peach Blueberry Pie**
Substitute 2 cups fresh or frozen peaches and 2 cups fresh or frozen blueberries for the apples.

**Variation:**
**Berry Sweetheart Pie**
Substitute 4 cups of mixed berries for the apples. Most grocery stores offer a frozen blend of strawberries, blackberries, raspberries and blueberries that works well in this recipe.

- In a large bowl, combine apples, coconut sugar, flour and spices. Spread apple mixture in bottom of panned crust. Dot apple mixture with cubes of butter.
- Roll remaining dough into a 12-inch circle. Loosely fold dough in half; gently lift and place fold across center of fruit filling. Unfold dough to cover filling. Lightly press together edges of top and bottom crusts; trim to ½ inch beyond pan's edge. Tuck under overhanging dough, even with pan's rim. Flute edge by placing thumb and index finger against the inside of the dough edge; press dough into the center of these fingers with other hand's index finger. Continue around entire edge of crust.

To finish the crust:

1 egg white, lightly beaten

1 teaspoon sugar

- Brush top of dough with egg white; sprinkle with 1 teaspoon sugar. Cut 3-5 slits in top crust, allowing steam to escape during baking.
- Bake at 400° for 15 minutes; lower oven to 350° and bake for additional 40-45 minutes or until top is golden. Cool for 1 hour before serving.

# Banana Cream Tart

**Yield: 9-inch tart**

*In this recipe, the crust is similar to a graham cracker crust and the filling is a made-from-scratch creamy pudding. They make an exceptional duo.*

For the crust:

1¾ cups Einkorn flour

2 tablespoons sugar

¼ teaspoon salt

8 tablespoons butter, melted

- In a medium bowl, combine flour, sugar and salt. Add melted butter; stir until dough holds together in a firm ball.
- Press dough into an even layer on the bottom and side of tart pan or pie plate. With a fork, generously prick the bottom and sides of the dough.
- Bake at 350° for 15-20 minutes or until lightly brown.

# Banana Cream Tart cont.

## Filling

**Variation: Chocolate Cream Tart**
Add ¼ cup cocoa powder to the dry ingredients for the filling. Garnish with chocolate curls in place of bananas.

**Tip:**
Use granulated sugar in place of coconut sugar if you prefer a creamy white filling.

For the filling:

⅓ cup coconut sugar

2 tablespoons Einkorn flour

2 tablespoons tapioca starch

2 eggs

14-ounce can unsweetened coconut milk
   OR 1¾ cup whole milk

2 tablespoons butter

1 teaspoon vanilla

1 banana, sliced

- In a small bowl, combine coconut sugar, flour and tapioca; set aside.
- In a medium bowl, lightly beat eggs; set aside.
- In medium saucepan over medium-low heat, warm milk just until bubbles form. Add dry ingredients, stirring constantly for 2 minutes until mixture thickens. Remove from heat and slowly add approximately ¼ of the hot mixture to beaten eggs, stirring thoroughly. Pour egg mixture into saucepan with hot milk mixture; mix well. Stirring constantly, heat mixture just until bubbles form again; reduce heat and cook 2 additional minutes. Remove from heat; stir in butter and vanilla. Cool slightly before pouring into baked tart crust.
- Refrigerate 30 minutes or until set. Garnish with sliced bananas before serving.

# Cakes & Cupcakes

Chocolate Whoopie Pies ................................................... 55

Banana Whoopie Pies ..................................................... 56

Pumpkin Whoopie Pies ................................................... 57

Vanilla Cupcakes .............................................................. 58

Chocolate Cupcakes ....................................................... 59

Mini Multigrain Bundt Cakes ....................................... 62

Orange Caramel Glaze ................................................... 63

Mini Lemon Pound Cake ............................................... 64

Berry Cake ........................................................................ 65

Carrot Cake ...................................................................... 66

Cream Cheese Frosting ................................................. 67

Strawberry Cream Cheese Frosting ........................... 68

Chocolate Buttercream Frosting ................................ 69

Peanut Butter Frosting ................................................. 70

# Chocolate Whoopie Pies

**Yield: 20 mini or 7 large pies**

*Not wanting to waste any ingredients, some women would bake their leftover batter into small mounds of cake and sandwich them together with a sweet creamy filling. Legend has it their husbands and children would yell "whoopie" when they found this treat in their lunch pails!*

**Filling Suggestions:**
Strawberry Cream Cheese Frosting (page 68)

Chocolate Buttercream Frosting (page 69)

Peanut Butter Frosting (page 70)

1 cup Einkorn flour
½ cup cocoa powder
½ teaspoon baking soda
½ teaspoon baking powder
½ teaspoon salt
¼ cup butter, softened
¼ cup coconut sugar
2 tablespoons honey
1 egg
1 teaspoon vanilla
½ cup buttermilk

- In a medium bowl, combine flour, cocoa powder, baking soda, baking powder and salt; set aside.
- In a bowl, using an electric mixer on medium speed, beat together butter, coconut sugar and honey. Scrape sides of bowl. Add egg; beat until light and fluffy. Add vanilla; mix well. Detach bowl from mixer. With a rubber spatula, alternately mix in dry ingredients and buttermilk, making two additions of each. Stir until smooth.
- Spoon batter into greased whoopie pan. Let batter rest 10 minutes.
- Bake at 350° for 6-8 minutes for mini cakes or 11-13 for large cakes, or until top of cake springs back when touched. Cool cakes in pan for 3 minutes; remove to wire rack to cool completely.
- Assemble pies: spread filling on one cake and sandwich with another cake.

# Banana Whoopie Pies

**Yield: 20 mini or 7 large pies**

*A fun name for a fun dessert! In this variation, ripe banana flavors the mini cakes. They are delicious with chocolate, cream cheese, or peanut butter filling.*

**Filling Suggestions:**
Chocolate Buttercream Frosting (page 69)
Peanut Butter Frosting (page 70)
Cream Cheese Frosting (page 67)

1 cup Einkorn flour
½ teaspoon baking soda
½ teaspoon baking powder
½ teaspoon salt
½ cup mashed ripe banana (1 medium)
¼ cup sour cream
¼ cup butter, softened
¼ cup coconut sugar
2 tablespoons honey
1 egg
1 teaspoon vanilla

- In a medium bowl, combine flour, baking soda, baking powder and salt; set aside.

- In a small bowl, combine mashed banana and sour cream; set aside.

- In a bowl, using an electric mixer on medium speed, beat together butter, coconut sugar and honey. Scrape sides of bowl. Add egg; beat until light and fluffy. Add vanilla; mix well. Detach bowl from mixer. With a rubber spatula, alternately mix in dry ingredients and banana mixture, making two additions of each. Stir until smooth.

- Spoon batter into greased whoopie pan. Let batter rest 10 minutes.

- Bake at 350° for 6-8 minutes for mini cakes or 11-13 for large cakes, or until top of cake springs back when touched. Cool cakes in pan for 3 minutes; remove to wire rack to cool completely.

- Assemble pies: spread filling on one cake and sandwich with another cake.

# Pumpkin Whoopie Pies

**Yield: 20 mini or 7 large pies**

*Don't let the name fool you! They are called pies, but they are really little cakes sandwiched together with a sweet creamy filling. This spiced pumpkin variety pairs well with cream cheese frosting.*

**Filling Suggestion:** Cream Cheese Frosting (page 67)

1 cup Einkorn flour
½ teaspoon baking soda
½ teaspoon baking powder
½ teaspoon salt
1 teaspoon cinnamon
½ teaspoon ginger
¼ teaspoon nutmeg
¼ teaspoon cloves

½ cup pumpkin puree
¼ cup sour cream or buttermilk
¼ cup butter, softened
¼ cup coconut sugar
2 tablespoons honey
1 egg
1 teaspoon vanilla

- In a medium bowl, combine flour, baking soda, baking powder, salt and spices; set aside.

- In a small bowl, combine pumpkin puree and sour cream or buttermilk; set aside.

- In a bowl, using an electric mixer on medium speed, beat together butter, coconut sugar and honey. Scrape sides of bowl. Add egg; beat until light and fluffy. Add vanilla; mix well. Detach bowl from mixer. With a rubber spatula, alternately mix in dry ingredients and pumpkin mixture, making two additions of each. Stir until smooth.

- Spoon batter into greased whoopie pan. Let batter rest 10 minutes.

- Bake at 350° for 6-8 minutes for mini cakes or 11-13 for large cakes, or until top of cake springs back when touched. Cool cakes in pan for 3 minutes; remove to wire rack to cool completely.

- Assemble pies: spread filling on one cake and sandwich with another cake.

# Vanilla Cupcakes

**Yield: 10-12 cupcakes**

*Cupcakes have become a popular dessert to celebrate special occasions. Their small size makes them easy to serve and provides portion control. Vanilla is a standard cake flavor that pairs well with many frostings.*

**Frosting Suggestions:**
Strawberry Cream Cheese Frosting (page 68)

Chocolate Buttercream Frosting (page 69)

Peanut Butter Frosting (page 70)

Cream Cheese Frosting (page 67)

1 cup Einkorn flour
1 teaspoon baking powder
¼ teaspoon salt
6 tablespoons butter, melted
¼ cup sour cream
1 teaspoon vanilla
2 eggs
⅓ cup sugar

- In a medium bowl, combine flour, baking powder and salt; set aside.
- In a small bowl, whisk melted butter, sour cream and vanilla; set aside.
- In a bowl, using an electric mixer on medium speed, beat eggs for 30 seconds. Add sugar and increase mixer to medium-high speed; beat for 1 minute. Detach bowl from mixer. With a rubber spatula, alternately mix in dry ingredients and butter mixture, making two additions of each. Stir until smooth.
- Spoon batter into paper-lined 2½-inch muffin cups, filling half full. Let batter rest 10 minutes.
- Bake at 350° for 15-18 minutes or until top of cake springs back when touched. Cool cupcakes in pan for 10 minutes; remove to wire rack to cool completely. Top cupcakes with frosting.

# Chocolate Cupcakes

**Yield: 10-12 cupcakes**

*You will find these chocolate cupcakes anything but basic when they are crowned with a creamy rich topping. Peanut Butter Frosting and Whipped Coconut Cream are two of my favorites for this cupcake.*

**Frosting Suggestions:**
Strawberry Cream Cheese Frosting (page 68)

Chocolate Buttercream Frosting (page 69)

Peanut Butter Frosting (page 70)

Cream Cheese Frosting (page 67)

¾ cup Einkorn flour

1 teaspoon baking powder

¼ teaspoon salt

5 tablespoons butter, melted

1 teaspoon vanilla

¼ cup cocoa powder

⅓ cup buttermilk

2 eggs

⅓ cup coconut sugar

- In a medium bowl, combine flour, baking powder and salt; set aside.
- In a small bowl, whisk melted butter, vanilla, cocoa powder and buttermilk; set aside.
- In a bowl, using an electric mixer on medium speed, beat eggs for 30 seconds. Add coconut sugar and increase mixer to medium-high speed; beat for 1 minute. Detach bowl from mixer. With a rubber spatula, alternately mix in dry ingredients and butter mixture, making two additions of each. Stir until smooth.
- Spoon batter into paper-lined 2½-inch muffin cups, filling half full. Let batter rest 10 minutes.
- Bake at 350° for 15-18 minutes or until top of cake springs back when touched. Cool cupcakes in pan for 10 minutes; remove to wire rack to cool completely. Top cupcakes with frosting.

Carrot Cake  p66

Berry Cake  p65

Mini Multigrain Cakes with Orange Caramel Glaze  p62

**Banana Whoopie Pies** p56
with Cream Cheese Frosting p67

**Vanilla Cupcakes** p58
with Strawberry Cream Cheese Icing p68

**Mini Lemon Pound Cake** p64

**Chocolate Cupcakes** p59
with Chocolate Buttercream Frosting p69

# Mini Multigrain Bundt Cakes

**Yield: 18 mini bundt cakes**

*The mini bundt was the signature shape for many of my shop's pastries. The design is unique and the size offers portion control. Orange Glaze is a wonderful topping for this pastry.*

1 cup Einkorn flour

1 cup almond flour

1½ teaspoon baking powder

¼ teaspoon baking soda

½ teaspoon salt

2 teaspoon orange zest

4 tablespoons butter, softened

¼ cup coconut sugar

2 tablespoons honey

2 eggs

¾ cup buttermilk

1 recipe Orange Caramel Glaze, page 63

- In a medium bowl, combine flours, baking powder, baking soda, salt and orange zest; set aside.
- In a bowl, using an electric mixer on medium speed, cream butter for 1 minute. Scrape sides of bowl and add coconut sugar and honey. Increase mixer to medium-high speed; mix for 1 minute. Add eggs; beat until light and fluffy. Detach bowl from mixer. With rubber spatula, alternately mix in dry ingredients and buttermilk, making two additions of each. Stir until smooth.
- Spoon batter into greased mini bundt pan, filling half full. Let batter rest 10 minutes.
- Bake at 350° for 15-20 minutes or until toothpick inserted near center comes out clean. Cool cakes in pan for 10 minutes; remove to wire rack. Drizzle with Orange Caramel Glaze.

# Orange Caramel Glaze

Yield: 18 mini bundt cakes

4 tablespoons butter
¼ cup coconut sugar
1 tablespoon water
2-3 drops orange essential oil

- In saucepan, melt butter over low heat. Add coconut sugar and water; whisk until blended. Heat mixture over medium-low heat until mixture begins to bubble. Reduce heat to low. Cook, stirring constantly, 3-4 minutes or until mixture has thickened. Transfer mixture to small bowl; stir in essential oil.
- Drizzle glaze when warm; the glaze will thicken while cooling.

# Mini Lemon Pound Cake

**Yield: 7-inch loaf**

A slice of pound cake is a standard menu item in coffee shops. Einkorn flour and coconut sugar make my recipe a better-for-you version. Lemon essential oil provides a bright flavor that enhances the sweetness of the coconut sugar and the citrus flavor of the zest.

1 cup Einkorn flour
1 teaspoon baking powder
¼ teaspoon salt
3 eggs
⅓ cup coconut sugar
2 teaspoon lemon zest
3-4 drops lemon essential oil
½ cup butter, melted

- In a medium bowl, combine flour, baking powder and salt; set aside.
- In a bowl, using an electric mixer on medium speed, beat eggs for 1 minute. Add coconut sugar, zest and essential oil; increase mixer to medium-high speed and beat for 1 minute. Slowly add melted butter; continue to mix for an additional minute. Detach bowl from mixer. With rubber spatula, mix in dry ingredients, half at a time. Stir until just combined.
- Spoon batter into greased loaf pan. Let batter rest 10 minutes.
- Bake at 350° for 25-30 minutes or until toothpick inserted near center comes out clean. Cool in pan on wire rack for 10 minutes. Remove loaf from pan; cool completely before slicing.

# Berry Cake

**Yield: 9-inch square cake**

*In this simple and quick one-layer cake recipe, Mother Nature's seasonal berries provide sweetness and beauty. Enjoy with a cup of coffee or a glass of milk.*

1½ cup Einkorn flour
1½ teaspoon baking powder
¼ teaspoon baking soda
¼ teaspoon salt
6 tablespoons butter, softened
¼ cup coconut sugar
2 tablespoons honey
2 eggs
½ cup sour cream
1 cup fresh or frozen berries
powdered sugar (optional)

- In a medium bowl, combine flour, baking powder, baking soda and salt; set aside.

- In a bowl, using an electric mixer on medium speed, cream butter for 1 minute. Scrape sides of bowl and add coconut sugar and honey; mix for 1 minute. Add eggs; beat until light and fluffy. Detach bowl from mixer. With rubber spatula, alternately mix in dry ingredients and sour cream, making two additions of each. Stir until smooth.

- Spoon batter into parchment paper-lined and lightly buttered 9-inch square pan. Let batter rest 10 minutes. Add berries on top.

- Bake at 350° for 25-35 minutes or until toothpick inserted near center comes out clean. Cool cake in pan for 15 minutes; remove to wire rack and carefully remove parchment paper. Before serving, dust with powdered sugar (optional).

# Carrot Cake

**Yield: 9-inch round cake**

*I have reformulated my shop's beloved carrot cake. Einkorn flour, olive oil, and coconut sugar make this version healthier than the original. The cake is moist with a dense texture, spiced with cinnamon and ginger and loaded with carrots, coconut, raisins, and nuts.*

- 1½ cup Einkorn flour
- ⅓ cup unsweetened flaked coconut
- 1 teaspoon baking powder
- ½ teaspoon baking soda
- ½ teaspoon salt
- 1 teaspoon cinnamon
- ¼ teaspoon ginger
- ¾ cup olive oil
- ½ cup raisins
- 2 cups grated carrots, divided
- 2 eggs
- ⅓ cup coconut sugar
- 1 teaspoon vanilla
- ½ cup chopped pecans
- 1 recipe cream cheese frosting, page 67 (optional)
- toasted coconut flakes (optional)

- In a medium bowl, combine flour, coconut, baking powder, baking soda, salt and spices; set aside.
- In a food processor, combine olive oil, raisins and 1 cup grated carrot; puree until raisins and carrot are finely chopped.
- In a bowl, using an electric mixer on medium speed, beat eggs for 1 minute. Add coconut sugar and vanilla; increase mixer to medium-high speed and beat for 1 minute. Detach bowl from mixer. With rubber spatula, alternately mix in dry ingredients and oil mixture, making two additions of each. Fold in remaining 1 cup grated carrots and nuts.
- Spoon batter into greased and floured 9-inch round cake pan. Let batter rest 10 minutes.
- Bake at 350° for 30-45 minutes or until toothpick inserted near center comes out clean. Cool cake in pan for 15 minutes; remove to wire rack to cool completely. Frost with Cream Cheese Frosting and decorate with toasted coconut flakes (optional).

# Cream Cheese Frosting

**Yield: 1¼ cup**

*This recipe has less powdered sugar than a traditional cream cheese frosting. With a creamy taste, smooth texture, and spreadable consistency, you'll be pleasantly surprised that you don't miss the eliminated sugar!*

8 ounces cream cheese, softened
6 tablespoons butter, softened
1 cup powdered sugar

- In a bowl, using an electric mixer on medium speed, cream together cream cheese and butter until light and fluffy. Scrape sides of bowl. Gradually add powdered sugar; beat well.

# Strawberry Cream Cheese Frosting

**Yield: 1 cup**

*Freeze-dried strawberries are a natural way to add color and flavor to this cream cheese frosting.*

½ cup freeze-dried strawberries, finely ground

4 ounces cream cheese, softened

4 tablespoons butter, softened

1½ cup powdered sugar

- In a bowl, using an electric mixer on medium speed, beat together cream cheese and butter until light and fluffy. Scrape sides of bowl. Gradually add ground freeze-dried strawberries and powdered sugar; beat well

# Chocolate Buttercream Frosting

**Yield: 1½ cups**

*This butter frosting offers a satisfying chocolate taste with less sugar. Cocoa powder provides a stiffer consistency suitable for spreading. If piping, you may need to blend in 1-2 teaspoons of milk.*

1¼ cup powdered sugar
2 tablespoons cocoa powder
12 tablespoons butter, softened

- In small bowl, combine powdered sugar and cocoa powder; set aside.
- In a bowl, using an electric mixer on medium speed, beat butter until light and fluffy. Scrape sides of bowl. Gradually add cocoa and powdered sugar mixture; beat well.

# Peanut Butter Frosting

**Yield: 1 cup**

*The great nutty flavor of peanut butter enables us to reduce the sugar in this recipe. This frosting is delicious atop a chocolate or vanilla cupcake and scrumptious sandwiched between two banana whoopie cakes.*

8 tablespoons butter, softened
¼ cup organic, no-sugar-added peanut butter
1 cup powdered sugar

- In a bowl, using an electric mixer on medium speed, cream together butter and peanut butter until light and fluffy. Scrape sides of bowl. Gradually add powdered sugar; beat well.

# Healthy Snacks & Bars

Granola ................................................................. 73

Multigrain Granola Bars ........................................ 74

Banana Bread Bars ................................................ 75

Crunchy Coconut Almond Bars ............................ 76

Peanut Butter Chickpea Blondies ........................ 79

Black Bean Peppermint Brownies ....................... 80

White Bean Pumpkin Bars .................................... 81

Cranberry Orange Energy Bites ........................... 82

Goji Berry Energy Bites ........................................ 83

Peanut Butter Oat Energy Bites ........................... 84

# Granola

**Yield: 8 cups**

*Oats, nuts, seeds and dried fruit make this a nutritious breakfast food or snack. The cinnamon bark and orange essential oils provide a signature flavor that makes you crave more.*

2 cups old-fashioned oats
¼ cup Einkorn flour
1 cup assorted nuts
1 cup pumpkin seeds
¼ cup sesame seeds
2 tablespoons chia seeds
2 tablespoons hemp seeds
⅓ cup honey
¼ cup coconut oil, melted
2 teaspoons vanilla
4-6 drops cinnamon bark essential oil or 1 tablespoon cinnamon
4-6 drops orange essential oil or zest of one orange
1 cup dried fruit
1 cup unsweetened flaked coconut
1 cup chocolate chips (optional)

- In a medium bowl, combine oats, flour, nuts and seeds; set aside.
- In a small bowl, combine honey, melted coconut oil, vanilla and essential oils. Pour mixture over dry ingredients; stir until pieces are thoroughly coated.
- Spread mixture evenly on parchment paper-lined baking sheet.
- Bake at 300° for 20 minutes. Remove pan from oven and stir. Continue to bake an additional 15-20 minutes, until golden brown. Let cool completely. Add dried fruit, coconut and chocolate chips (optional).
- Store in an airtight container.

# Multigrain Granola Bars

**Yield: 12 bars**

*These chewy bars contain Einkorn's beneficial nutrients and are loaded with healthy nuts, seeds, and dried fruits. They are a perfect after school snack!*

**Tip:**
Taking time to firmly press granola into the pan before baking and letting it cool 1-2 hours before cutting is key to yielding a bar that will hold together.

2 cups old-fashioned oats
½ cup Einkorn flour
2 tablespoons coconut sugar
½ cup nuts (almonds, walnuts or pecans), coarsely chopped
½ cup dried fruit (raisins, cranberries or goji berries)
¼ cup large seeds (pumpkin or sunflower)
1 tablespoon small seeds (flax, sesame or chia)
¼ cup unsweetened flaked coconut or chocolate chips
¼ cup olive oil
¼ cup butter, melted and cooled
⅓ cup honey

- In a large bowl, combine oats, flour, sugars, nuts, dried fruit, seeds and coconut or chocolate chips.
- Add the olive oil to the dry ingredients and mix to distribute. Let rest 5 minutes.
- In a small bowl, combine butter and honey: blend well. Pour mixture over the granola mixture and stir until thoroughly combined.
- Spread mixture into a parchment paper-lined 9-inch square baking pan. Use a rubber spatula or damp finger tips to firmly press the granola into the pan.
- Bake at 325° for 30 minutes. Cool completely before removing from pan and cutting into bars

# Banana Bread Bars

**Yield: 16 bars**

*Healthy multigrain breakfast bars that taste like banana bread. They are easy to make and even easier to eat!*

For the bars:
- ¾ cup old-fashioned oats, finely ground
- ¾ cup Einkorn flour
- ¾ cup almond flour
- ½ teaspoon baking powder
- ½ teaspoon baking soda
- ¼ teaspoon salt
- 1 teaspoon cinnamon
- 3 medium ripe bananas
- ¼ cup applesauce
- ¼ cup honey
- 2 teaspoons vanilla
- ⅓ cup chocolate chips

- In a large bowl, combine ground oats, flours, baking powder, baking soda, salt and cinnamon; set aside
- In a food processor, place bananas, applesauce, honey and vanilla; blend until smooth and creamy. Add banana mixture to dry ingredients and stir until just combined. Fold in chocolate chips.
- Spread batter in a parchment paper-lined 9-inch square baking pan. Let batter rest 10 minutes.
- Bake at 350° for 20-25 minutes or until toothpick inserted near center comes out clean. Cool on wire rack for 15 minutes before removing from pan.

For chocolate topping:
- 2 tablespoons chocolate chips
- ½ teaspoon coconut oil

- Combine 2 tablespoons chocolate chips and coconut oil in small bowl and microwave for 30 seconds or until melted; stir well. Drizzle over bars. Cool completely before cutting into bars.

# Crunchy Coconut Almond Bars

**Yield: 14 bars**

*A subtle almond flavor and crunchy texture make this snack bar reminiscent of biscotti.*

½ cup old-fashioned oats
½ cup Einkorn flour
½ cup unsweetened flaked coconut
¼ cup almonds, coarsely chopped
¼ cup pecans, coarsely chopped
¼ cup sesame seeds
¼ cup sunflower seeds
¼ cup dates or raisins
¾ cup tahini
½ cup honey
½ teaspoon almond extract

- In a large bowl, combine oats, flour, coconut, nuts, seeds and fruit; set aside.
- In a small bowl, combine tahini and honey; heat in microwave for 1 minute. Add almond extract; blend well. Pour mixture over dry ingredients and stir until thoroughly combined.
- Place dough onto a parchment paper-lined baking sheet. With damp hands, press into a 5x7-inch rectangle. Let dough rest 10 minutes.
- Bake at 350° for 20-25 minutes or until edges are golden brown; center will feel soft, but will firm up as it cools. Cool completely before cutting into bars.

Granola  p73

Peanut Butter Chickpea Blondies  p79

Banana Bread Bars  p75

Black Bean Peppermint Brownies  p80

Left to right:
Peanut Butter Oat Energy Bites  p84
Cranberry Orange Energy Bites  p82
Gojiberry Energy Bites  p83

Multigrain Granola Bars  p74

# Peanut Butter Chickpea Blondies

**Yield: 16 bars**

*Packed with protein, chickpeas secretly make these bars healthy. These bars taste surprisingly like peanut butter cookies.*

⅓ cup Einkorn flour
2 tablespoons coconut sugar
½ teaspoon baking powder
¼ teaspoon salt
15-ounce can chickpeas, drained and rinsed
¼ cup maple syrup
½ cup organic, no-sugar-added peanut butter
1 teaspoon vanilla
2 tablespoons butter, melted
½ cup chocolate chips

- In a large bowl, combine flour, coconut sugar, baking powder and salt; set aside.
- In a food processor, blend chickpeas until smooth. Add maple syrup, peanut butter, vanilla and melted butter; mix until creamy. Pour mixture over dry ingredients and stir until just combined. Fold in chocolate chips.
- Spread batter in a parchment paper-lined 9-inch square baking pan. Let batter rest 10 minutes.
- Bake at 350° for 20-25 minutes or until toothpick inserted near center comes out clean. Cool on wire rack for 15 minutes before removing from pan. Cool completely before cutting into bars.

# Black Bean Peppermint Brownies

**Yield: 16 bars**

*No one will believe these delicious brownies are made with black beans! This legume adds color, texture, and nutrition to this recipe.*

½ cup Einkorn flour

½ teaspoon baking powder

¼ teaspoon salt

15-ounce can black beans, drained and rinsed

¼ cup cocoa powder

⅓ cup coconut sugar

¼ cup butter, melted

3 eggs, lightly beaten

2 teaspoons vanilla

4-6 drops peppermint essential oil

¾ cups chocolate chips

2 tablespoons cacao nibs, for decoration

- In a large bowl, combine flour, baking powder and salt; set aside.
- In a food processor, blend black beans until smooth. Add cocoa powder, coconut sugar, melted butter, eggs, vanilla and essential oil; mix until creamy. Pour mixture over dry ingredients and stir until just combined. Fold in chocolate chips.
- Spread batter in a parchment paper-lined 9-inch square baking pan. Sprinkle cacao nibs on top. Let batter rest 10 minutes.
- Bake at 350° for 20-25 minutes or until toothpick inserted near center comes out clean. Cool on wire rack for 15 minutes before removing from pan. Cool completely before cutting into bars

# White Bean Pumpkin Bars

**Yield: 16 bars**

*A quick and easy recipe containing vitamin-rich pumpkin puree and protein-packed white beans. This bar is sure to become one of your family's favorite snacks!*

15-ounce can white bean (northern, cannelloni or navy), rinsed and drained

½ cup pumpkin puree

2 medium ripe bananas

¼ cup coconut sugar

2 tablespoons maple syrup or honey

2 tablespoons organic, no-sugar-added peanut butter

2 drops cinnamon bark essential oil

2 drops nutmeg essential oil

1 drop clove essential oil

½ cup Einkorn flour

½ cup chocolate chips (optional)

½ cup nuts (optional)

- In a food processor, place beans, pumpkin puree, bananas, coconut sugar, maple syrup or honey, peanut butter and essential oils; blend until smooth and creamy. Add flour; stir until just combined. Fold in chocolate chips or nuts (optional).
- Spread batter in a parchment paper-lined 9-inch square baking pan. Let batter rest 10 minutes.
- Bake at 350° for 20-25 minutes or until toothpick inserted near center comes out clean. Cool on wire rack for 15 minutes before removing from pan. Cool completely before cutting into bars.

# Cranberry Orange Energy Bites

Yield: 12-24 bites

*Rolled into bite-sized spheres and coated with decorative coconut, this fruity no-bake dough becomes a healthy alternative to a truffle.*

**Variation:
Key Lime Pie Energy Bites**
Substitute 1 cup macadamia nuts for sliced almonds, ½ cup raisins for dried cranberries and 4-6 drops lime essential oil for orange essential oil. Coat with green Natural Rainbow Sprinkles (page 15).

**Variation:
Lemon Macaroon Energy Bites**
Substitute ½ cup raisins for dried cranberries and 4-6 drops lemon essential oil for orange essential oil. Coat with yellow Natural Rainbow Sprinkles (page 15).

1 cup sliced almonds

½ cup dried cranberries

1 tablespoon water

3 tablespoons protein powder

½ cup desiccated coconut plus 2 tablespoon for coating

4-6 drops orange essential oil

- In a food processor, place sliced almonds; pulse until finely ground. Add dried cranberries and water; blend until well combined. Add protein powder, coconut and essential oil; continue to blend until mixture begins to form a ball.

- On a parchment paper-lined baking sheet, firmly press dough into a 6x4-inch rectangle approximately ½ inch thick. Refrigerate for 2 hours. Cut into 24 1-inch squares or divide dough into 12 equal portions; roll into balls. Coat with desiccated coconut.

- Store room temperature in an airtight container.

# Goji Berry Energy Bites

**Yield: 18-36 bites**

*Pop one into your mouth to refuel after a big game or tough workout!*

½ cup pumpkin seeds

¼ cup sesame seeds

¼ cup sunflower seeds

2 tablespoons chia seeds

3 tablespoons protein powder

2 tablespoons cocoa powder

¼ cup old-fashioned oats

2 tablespoons goji berries

8 dates

¼ cup coconut oil

- Place all ingredients in food processor; pulse until ingredients are well blended and mixture begins to form a ball.
- On a parchment paper-lined baking sheet, firmly press dough into a 6-inch square approximately ½ inch thick. Refrigerate for 2 hours. Cut into 36 1-inch squares or divide dough into 18 equal portions; roll into balls.
- Store room temperature in an airtight container.

# Peanut Butter Oat Energy Bites

**Yield: 18-36 bites**

*Looking for a healthy snack? Try making these no-bake morsels that taste like a peanut butter cookie. Protein powder, chia seeds, and cacao nibs add nutritional value to this easy-to-make snack.*

3 tablespoons protein powder
1 cup old-fashioned oats
2 tablespoons chia seeds
2 tablespoons cacao nibs
6 dates
2½ tablespoons water
3 tablespoons maple syrup or honey
1 tablespoon vanilla
2/3 cup organic, no-sugar-added peanut butter

- In a medium bowl, combine protein powder, oats, chia seeds and cacao nibs; set aside.
- In a food processor, place dates and water; pulse until paste-like consistency is achieved. Add maple syrup or honey, vanilla and peanut butter; blend well.
- On a parchment paper-lined baking sheet, firmly press dough into a 6-inch square approximately ½ inch thick; refrigerate for 2 hours. Cut into 36 1-inch squares or divide dough into 18 equal portions; roll into balls.
- Store room temperature in an airtight container.

# Miscellaneous Fun

Brownie Bark ............................................................................ 87

Cinnamon Coconut Crisp Cereal ........................................... 88

Cinnamon Oatmeal Pancakes ................................................ 91

Artichoke, Tomato & Spinach Einkorn Pizza ........................ 92

Graham Crackers .................................................................... 94

Cheddar Star Crackers ........................................................... 95

Sesame Rosemary Crackers .................................................. 96

Cream Puffs ............................................................................. 97

Whipped Coconut Cream ...................................................... 98

Real Chocolate Bits ................................................................ 99

# Brownie Bark

**Yield: 36 pieces**

*Beyond the title, this recipe needs little explanation. The brownie is fudgy and has a bark-like crunch. Warning: will become addictive!*

½ cup chocolate chips
2½ tablespoons coconut oil
2 tablespoons cocoa powder
2 egg whites
½ cup sugar
6 tablespoons Einkorn flour
¼ teaspoon baking soda
¼ teaspoon salt
⅓ cup cacao nibs

- In a small bowl, combine chocolate chips, coconut oil and cocoa powder. Heat in microwave for 1 minute or until chocolate is melted; set aside and let cool.
- In another small bowl, beat egg whites until frothy; set aside.
- In a large bowl, combine sugar, flour, baking soda and salt. Add melted chocolate mixture and stir until well blended. Fold in egg whites.
- On a parchment paper-lined baking sheet, pour half of the batter and spread to ⅛-inch thickness. Repeat with remaining batter on another parchment paper-lined baking sheet. Sprinkle cacao nibs on top of batter. Let batter rest 10 minutes.
- Bake at 325° for 10 minutes; rotate pans and bake another 10 minutes. Remove pans from oven. With a sharp knife or pizza cutter, cut brownie bark into 2-inch squares. Return pans to oven and bake an additional 5 minutes. Cool completely; break into pieces.
- Store in an airtight container.

# Cinnamon Coconut Crisp Cereal

**Yield: 3¾ cups**

This is the perfect snack to have in your purse or backpack. This snack is easy to carry and easy to eat. Of course, great for breakfast too! Serve with milk and fresh fruit.

**Tip:**
1½ teaspoons of cinnamon can be used in place of cinnamon bark essential oil. Combine the cinnamon with the dry ingredients.

½ cup Einkorn flour
½ cup almond flour
½ cup flaxseed meal
½ cup unsweetened shredded coconut
¼ teaspoon baking soda
¼ teaspoon salt
1 egg white
1 tablespoon coconut oil, melted
2 tablespoons honey
6 drops cinnamon bark essential oil

- In a large bowl, combine flours, flaxseed meal, coconut, baking soda and salt; set aside.
- In a small bowl, beat egg white until frothy; set aside.
- In another small bowl, combine melted coconut oil, honey and essential oil. Add frothy egg white and blend. Add liquid mixture to dry ingredients; stir until ingredients are well blended and mixture begins to form a ball. Let dough rest 10 minutes.
- Place half of the dough on a piece of parchment paper; cover with another piece of parchment paper. Roll dough to 1/16-inch thickness; remove top piece of parchment paper. Leave rolled-dough on parchment paper; slide onto baking sheet. With a sharp knife or pizza cutter, cut dough into ¾-inch squares. Repeat with remaining dough.
- Bake at 350° for 12-15 minutes or until golden brown. Cool completely; break into pieces.
- Store in an airtight container.

**Graham Crackers** p94

**Cinnamon Coconut Crisp Cereal** p88

**Cheddar Star Crackers** p95
**Sesame Rosemary Crackers** p96

**Brownie Bark** p87

Cinnamon Oatmeal Pancakes  p91

Cream Puff  p97
with Whipped Coconut Cream  p98

Real Chocolate Bits  p99

# Cinnamon Oatmeal Pancakes

**Yield: 12 pancakes**

*I used a large whoopie pan to create mini-cakes that bake and freeze well. Pop them into the toaster for a warm breakfast when you're short on time.*

**Tip:**
½ teaspoons of cinnamon can be used in place of cinnamon bark essential oil. Combine the cinnamon with the dry ingredients.

¾ cup Einkorn flour
¼ cup old-fashioned oats, coarsely ground
1 teaspoon baking powder
½ teaspoon baking soda
¼ teaspoon salt
1 tablespoon coconut oil, melted
2 tablespoon honey
1 egg, lightly beaten
¾ cup buttermilk
1 tablespoon vanilla
2 drops cinnamon bark essential oil

- In a large bowl combine, flour, ground oats, baking powder, baking soda and salt; set aside.
- In a small bowl, combine melted coconut oil, honey, egg, buttermilk, vanilla and essential oil. Pour mixture over dry ingredients and whisk until batter is smooth.
- Spoon batter into greased large whoopie pan. Let batter rest 10 minutes.
- Bake at 400° for 5-7 minutes until top of cake springs back when touched. Cool cakes in pan for 3 minutes; remove to wire rack to cool completely.

# Artichoke, Tomato & Spinach Einkorn Pizza

**Yield: 12-inch pizza**

*Once you discover how wonderful this pizza tastes, you'll never want to eat a commercial one again. Customize the Einkorn pizza crust with your choice of toppings. Crusts can be made ahead and frozen for a future quick and easy meal.*

**Tip:**
Dough can be frozen after rolled. When ready to use, remove from freezer, defrost and let rise before topping and baking.

For the crust:

½ cup warm water

1 teaspoon active dry yeast

1 teaspoon honey

1½ cup Einkorn flour

½ teaspoon salt

1½ teaspoon olive oil

- In a small bowl, combine water, yeast and honey; let rest at room temperature for 10 minutes. Mixture will become bubbly and frothy.
- In a large bowl combine flour and salt. Add yeast mixture and olive oil to dry ingredients; stir until ingredients are combined. With hands, continue to mix and press dough until smooth. Let dough rest 10 minutes.
- On a piece of parchment paper, use hands to press dough into a 12-inch circle. Leave rolled-dough on parchment paper; slide onto baking sheet. Let dough rise in warm place for 45-50 minutes.

Continued on page 93.

# Artichoke, Tomato & Spinach Einkorn Pizza cont.

Yield: 12-inch pizza

For the topping:

5 tablespoon olive oil

3 garlic cloves, finely chopped

3 tablespoons chopped parsley

salt

pepper

2 cups shredded mozzarella cheese

5 tablespoon grated Parmesan cheese, divided

13.75-ounce can artichoke hearts, drained and quartered

½ pint grape tomatoes, halved

2 cups baby spinach, chopped

- In a small bowl, combine olive oil, garlic and parsley; season with salt and pepper. Spread 2 tablespoons of garlic mixture onto proofed, unbaked crust.
- Sprinkle mozzarella cheese and 2 tablespoons Parmesan cheese on top of oiled crust.
- Toss artichokes hearts, tomatoes and spinach with remaining garlic mixture; arrange on top of cheese. Sprinkle with remaining 3 tablespoons Parmesan cheese.
- Bake at 450° for 12-15 minutes. Let cool 5 minutes and cut into slices.

# Graham Crackers

**Yield: 10 crackers**

*These taste and look like store-bought graham crackers. Crush them to use in your favorite graham cracker crust recipe.*

1 cup Einkorn flour
¼ teaspoon baking powder
¼ teaspoon baking soda
¼ teaspoon salt
3 tablespoon butter, melted
2 tablespoons honey
1 tablespoon water
1 teaspoon sugar, for decoration

- In a large bowl, combine flour, baking powder, baking soda and salt; set aside.
- In a small bowl, combine melted butter, honey and water. Add to dry ingredients; stir until ingredients are well blended and mixture begins to form a ball. Let dough rest 10 minutes.
- Place dough on a piece of parchment paper; cover with another piece of parchment paper. Roll dough to ⅛-inch thickness; remove top piece of parchment paper. Leave rolled-dough on parchment paper; slide onto baking sheet. With a sharp knife or pizza cutter, cut dough into 2-inch squares. Prick each square with a fork.
- Bake at 350° for 15 minutes or until golden brown. Remove from oven. Lower oven temperature to 200°; bake an additional 5-10 minutes until crackers are crisp. Cool completely; break into pieces.
- Store in an airtight container.

# Cheddar Star Crackers

**Yield: 70-80 crackers**

*Impress your family and friends with these homemade crackers. They are so delicious that they are worth the time needed to make them.*

**Tip:**
¼ teaspoon of ground black pepper can be used in place of black pepper essential oil.

1 cup Einkorn flour
¼ cup almond flour
¼ teaspoon baking soda
1 teaspoon salt
1 cup finely grated cheddar cheese
1 tablespoon olive oil
1 egg, lightly beaten
2 drops black pepper essential oil

- In a food processor, place flours, baking soda and salt; blend. Add cheese, olive oil, egg and essential oil; pulse until ingredients are well blended and mixture begins to form a ball. Let dough rest 10 minutes.

- On lightly floured piece of parchment paper, place half of the dough; cover with another piece of parchment paper. Roll dough to ⅛-inch thickness; remove top piece of parchment paper. Cut dough with 1½-inch star cookie cutter. Gently lift cutout dough and place ½ inch apart onto parchment paper-lined baking sheets. Repeat with remaining dough.

- Bake at 350° for 15 minutes or until golden. Remove from oven. Lower oven temperature to 200°; bake an additional 5-10 minutes until crackers are crisp. Cool completely.

- Store in an airtight container.

# Sesame Rosemary Crackers

**Yield: 60-70 crackers**

*Make a batch of these to stock your pantry. They are satisfying when you crave a savory crunchy snack.*

**Tip:**
1 teaspoon minced fresh rosemary, ½ teaspoon dried rosemary or ½ teaspoon Italian seasoning can be used in place of rosemary essential oil.

1 cup Einkorn flour
½ cup sesame seeds
1 tablespoon chia seeds
1 tablespoon flax seeds
1 teaspoon garlic powder
1 teaspoon salt
2 tablespoons olive oil
1 tablespoon water
1 egg, lightly beaten
3-4 drops rosemary essential oil

- In a large bowl, combine flour, seeds, garlic powder and salt. Add olive oil, water, egg and essential oil; stir until mixture begins to form a ball. With hands, continue to mix and press dough until smooth. Let dough rest 10 minutes.

- Place dough on a piece of parchment paper; cover with another piece of parchment paper. Roll dough to $1/8$-inch thickness; remove top piece of parchment paper. Leave rolled-dough on parchment paper; slide onto baking sheet. With a knife or pizza cutter, cut dough into 1-inch squares.

- Bake at 400° for 15 minutes or until golden. Remove from oven. Lower oven temperature to 200°; bake an additional 5-10 minutes until crackers are crisp. Cool completely; break into pieces.

- Store in an airtight container.

# Cream Puffs

**Yield: 24 mini cream puffs**

*My shop sweetened many lives with the thousands of cream puffs we made for a local festival. Making them bite-size allows you to savor the flavor without a sugar overload!*

**Tip:**
Store unfilled puffs in a brown paper bag. They will get soggy if stored in plastic.

**Variation:**
**Éclair Puffs**
In place of Whipped Coconut Cream, fill sliced puffs with Cream Filling (page 52) and drizzle with Chocolate Glaze (page 28).

**Variation:**
**Savory Sandwich Puffs**
In place of Whipped Coconut Cream, fill sliced puffs with your favorite savory salad (chicken, tuna or ham).

1 cup all-purpose Einkorn flour (all-purpose is the only type that yields desirable results)

½ tablespoon coconut sugar

¼ teaspoon salt

¼ cup butter

½ cup water

3 eggs

½ teaspoon vanilla

1 recipe Whipped Coconut Cream, page 98

- In a medium bowl, combine flour, coconut sugar and salt; set aside.
- In a small saucepan over medium heat, bring butter and water to a boil. Remove from heat and add dry ingredients; stir until ingredients are well combined and form a pasty batter. Transfer batter to a bowl; with an electric mixer, beat in one egg at a time. Mix in vanilla.
- Drop batter by rounded spoonfuls 1 inch apart onto parchment paper-lined baking sheets. Let batter rest 10 minutes.
- Bake at 425° for 20-22 minutes or until golden. Cool completely before slicing and filling with Whipped Coconut Cream (page 98).

# Whipped Coconut Cream

**Yield: 2 cups**

*An easy-to-make vegan whipped cream used to fill pastry puffs, which is also a great topping for cupcakes and pies.*

**Variation:
Berry Whipped Coconut Cream**
Fold in ½ cup of freeze-dried fruit that has been finely ground.

**Variation:
Chocolate Whipped Coconut Cream**
Add 2 tablespoons of cocoa powder with the powdered sugar before mixing.

14-ounce can coconut cream, chilled in refrigerator overnight
¼ to ½ cup sugar or powdered sugar
½ teaspoon vanilla

- Place empty mixing bowl in refrigerator; chill for 10 minutes.
- Remove coconut cream from refrigerator. Without tipping or shaking, remove lid and spoon out thickened cream that has separated from the liquid on the bottom of the can. Place cream in chilled mixing bowl. Add sugar or powdered sugar and vanilla. With an electric mixer on low speed, whip until sugar and vanilla have dissolved. Increase mixer speed to high; continue to whip until mixture is creamy and smooth.
- Use immediately or refrigerate up to 1 week. Mixture will thicken slightly.

# Real Chocolate Bits

**Yield: 18 bits**

*At my shop, we had hundreds of molds that we used to shape confectionery coating into decorative bits. As a healthier alternative, I am delighted to share this simple recipe that uses natural raw cacao butter and cacao powder.*

2 ounces cacao butter

3 tablespoons raw cacao powder

2 tablespoons coconut sugar

1 teaspoon vanilla

pinch sea salt

1 drop peppermint essential oil (optional)

1 to 2 tablespoon finely chopped nuts (optional)

1 to 2 tablespoon unsweetened shredded coconut (optional)

pinch chili powder (optional)

- In a small saucepan over very low heat, slowly melt cacao butter. Remove from heat; stir in remaining ingredients.
- Spoon chocolate mixture into silicone molds with 1-inch cavities. Chill in refrigerator for 30-45 minutes until chocolate is firm. Gently tap chocolate bits out of candy mold.
- Store room temperature in an airtight container.

# Acknowledgments

### To Dr. Sandy,

Thank you for welcoming me to *Ager Chiropractic Wellness Center*. I value the support and confidence you have given me. I could always count on you and your staff to willingly sample and critique every bakery item I brought to you.

### To Clara,

You won't remember this when you are able to read, but you were so eager to sample every creation I gave to you. If it was "Clara Approved," I knew I had a winner!

### To Ellen,

Your encouragement fueled me to keep learning, baking, teaching, and sharing as much as I could. I am so grateful that you empowered me to cultivate my true passion. Your coaching has awakened me to a whole new level of possibilities!

### To Monica,

Your classes inspired me to pursue the writing of this cookbook. Your enthusiasm for me to create recipes for your sessions resulted in my determination to reformulate my family's favorite recipes. Thank you for being such a wonderful role model and mentor.

### To Annette,

I could not have done this without your willingness to join me in this venture. You tested every recipe and wrote the explicit directions for them. You then staged each bakery item and took wonderful photographs that made the recipes come to life. I have so such appreciation for all the countless hours you spent baking and editing each and every page. I am indeed grateful to have such a talented and dedicated daughter!

### To Lisa,

You so willingly offered to provide a second set of eyes in editing the final drafts. I appreciate all your time and effort. I value the feedback you gave to this project. I am fortunate to have a daughter-in-law that takes an interest in my endeavors!

### To Larry,

You were always eager to taste everything I made. Even though some of the trials were not so great, you faithfully gave honest and constructive critiques. Thank you for believing in me and allowing me to follow my dreams. I am blessed to have such a supportive husband!

### To Friends and Neighbors,

I appreciate your willingness to sample my recipes and to let my creations be the topic of every conversation. Even though some of my first attempts were questionable, I thank you for your interest and feedback.

### To Deb,

Your graphic design and artistic talents are amazing. Your patience and willingness to edit and re-edit recipes and other content is greatly appreciated. Thank you for guiding me through the book writing and self-publishing process. I am indeed grateful for your friendship!

# *-Index-*

**-A-**

Artichoke, Tomato & Spinach Einkorn Pizza, 92

**-B-**

**Banana:**

...Banana Bread, 19

...Banana Bread Bars, 75

...Banana Cream Tart, 51

...Banana Whoopie Pies, 56

**Bars:**

...Banana Bread Bars, 75

...Black Bean Peppermint Brownies, 80

...Crunchy Coconut Almond Bars, 76

...Multigrain Granola Bars, 74

...Peanut Butter Chickpea Blondies, 79

...White Bean Pumpkin Bars, 81

**Breads:**

...Banana Bread, 19

...Classic Wheat Bread, 31

...Multigrain Einkorn Bread, 33

...Pumpkin Bread, 21

...Zucchini Bread, 20

Breakfast Scones, 29

**Brownies:**

...Black Bean Peppermint Brownies, 80

...Brownie Bark, 87

**-C-**

**Cakes:**

...Berry Cake, 65

...Carrot Cake, 66

...Chocolate Cupcakes, 59

...Mini Lemon Pound Cake, 64

...Mini Multigrain Bundt Cakes, 62

...Vanilla Cupcakes, 58

**Carrot:**

...Carrot Cake, 66

...Morning Glory Muffins, 24

**Chocolate:**

...Chocolate Buttercream Frosting, 69

...Chocolate Chip Cookies, 1

...Chocolate Cupcakes, 59

...Chocolate Glaze, 28

...Chocolate Whoopie Pies, 55

...Double Chocolate Cookies, 7

...Real Chocolate Bits, 99

**Cinnamon:**

...Cinnamon Bark Honey Bears, 13

...Cinnamon Coconut Crisp Cereal, 88

...Cinnamon Oatmeal Pancakes, 91

...Cinnamon Rolls, 35

**Cookies:**

...Chocolate Chip, 1

...Cinnamon Bark Honey Bears, 13

...Double Chocolate, 7

...Ginger Snaps, 6

...Oatmeal Raisin, 2

...Party Time, 10

...Peanut Butter, 8

...Snickerdoodles, 3

...Snowballs, 9

...Sugar Cookie Cutouts, 11

**Coconut:**

...Crunchy Coconut Almond Bars, 76

...Whipped Coconut Cream, 98

**Crackers:**

...Cheddar Star Crackers, 95

...Graham Crackers, 94

...Sesame Rosemary Crackers, 96

Cream Puffs, 97

**-D-**

Donuts, 27

Double Chocolate Cookies, 7

**-F-**

**Frostings:**

...Chocolate Buttercream Frosting, 69

...Chocolate Glaze, 28

...Cinnamon Roll Icing, 37

...Cream Cheese Frosting, 67

...Orange Caramel Glaze, 63

...Peanut Butter Frosting, 70

...Powdered Sugar Frosting, 12

...Strawberry Frosting, 68

...Whipped Coconut Cream, 98

...White Glaze, 28

**-G-**

Galette, Blueberry, 41

Glaze, Chocolate, 28

Glaze, Orange Caramel, 63

Glaze, White, 28

Goji Berry Energy Bites, 83

Graham Crackers, 94

Granola, 73

Granola Bars, Multigrain, 74

**-L-**

Lemon, Mini Pound Cake, 64

**-M-**

Morning Glory Muffins, 24

Muffins, 25

**Multigrain:**

...Multigrain Einkorn Bread, 33

...Multigrain Granola Bars, 74

...Multigrain Mini Bundt Cakes, 62

**-N-**

Natural Rainbow Sprinkles, 15

**-O-**

Orange Caramel Glaze, 63

**-P-**

Pancakes, Cinnamon Oatmeal, 91

**Peanut Butter:**

...Peanut Butter Chickpea Blondies, 79

...Peanut Butter, Cookies, 8

...Peanut Butter Frosting, 70

...Peanut Butter Oat Energy Bites, 84

**Pies:**

...Apple Crumble Pie, 47

...Banana Whoopie Pies, 56

...Chocolate Whoopie Pies, 55

...Classic Apple Pie, 49

...Pumpkin Pie, 45

...Pumpkin Whoopie Pies, 57

Pizza, Artichoke, Tomato & Spinach, 92

Pound Cake, Lemon, 64

**Pumpkin:**

...Pumpkin Bars, White Bean, 81

...Pumpkin Bread, 21

...Pumpkin Pie, 45

...Pumpkin Whoopie Pie, 57

**-R-**

Rainbow Natural Sprinkles, 15

**-S-**

Scones, Breakfast, 29

**Snacks:**

...Banana Bread Bars, 75

...Black Bean Peppermint Brownies, 80

...Cranberry Orange Energy Bites, 82

...Crunchy Almond Bars, 76

...Goji Berry Energy Bites, 83

...Granola, 73

...Multigrain Granola Bars, 74

...Peanut Butter Chickpea Blondies, 79

...Peanut Butter Oat Energy Bites, 84

...White Bean Pumpkin Bars, 81

Sprinkles, Natural Rainbow, 15

Strawberry Cream Cheese Frosting, 68

**-T-**

Tart, Banana Cream, 51

**-V-**

Vanilla Glaze, 28

**-W-**

Whipped Coconut Cream, 98

**Whoopie Pies:**

...Banana Whoopie Pies, 56

...Chocolate Whoopie Pies, 55

...Pumpkin Whoopie Pies, 57

# Notes

# Notes

# Notes